Stimulus and Response

Stimulus AND Response

JOHN A. BARLOW

Hope College, Holland, Michigan

HARPER & ROW, PUBLISHERS

New York, Evanston, and London

Stimulus and Response

LIBRARY OF CONGRESS CATALOG CARD NUMBER: 68-10140

For Aaron, Joel, and Michael

Crafty men contemn studies, simple men admire them, and wise men use them; for they teach not their own use; but that is a wisdom without them and above them, won by observation. Read not to contradict and confute, nor to believe and take for granted, nor to find talk and discourse, but to weigh and consider.

—FRANCIS BACON, "Of Studies," 1597.

. . . What facts are there which are actually observed and studied by the psychologist and which do not fall wholly within the province of any other science? The answer must be twofold; namely, (1) his own consciousness, and (2) the behavior of men and of animals in general.

. . . .

We may then define psychology as the positive science of the behaviour of living things. To accept this definition is to return to the standpoint of Aristotle, and to set out from generally recognized facts, unprejudiced by theories.

—WILLIAM McDOUGALL, *Psychology, The Study of Behaviour* (New York: Henry Holt and Company, 1912), p. 19.

Crafty men contemn studies, simple men admire them, and wise men use them; for they teach not their own use; but that is a wisdom without them and above them, won by observation. Read not to contradict and confute, nor to believe and take for granted, nor to find talk and discourse, but to weigh and consider.

—FRANCIS BACON, "Of Studies," 1597.

. . . What facts are there which are actually observed and studied by the psychologist and which do not fall wholly within the province of any other science? The answer must be twofold, namely, (1) his own consciousness and (2) the behavior of men and of animals in general.

We may then define psychology as the positive science of the behaviour of living things. To accept this definition is to return to the standpoint of Aristotle, and to set out from generally recognized facts, unprejudiced by theories.

—WILLIAM McDOUGALL, *Psychology, The Study of Behaviour* (New York: Henry Holt and Company, 1912) p. 19.

Contents

Preface

> **Training in psychology will not make good teachers; but there is no doubt that good teachers can be better for an acquaintance with the general psychology of learning.**
>
> **—E. R. GUTHRIE[1]**

This book teaches one of the oldest theories of learning. The book can be mastered in six or seven hours of study. It is not an alternative to any textbook. It is not, furthermore, a substitute for chapters or a chapter in any other book. It is intended as a unique supplement for courses in Educational Psychology, General Psychology, and Learning.

The theory is the ancient contiguity theory. The bases for the development are (1) Virginia Voeks' formalization of E. R. Guthrie's version of the theory; (2) careful formulation of various usages of the term "stimulus" and of B. F. Skinner's operant-respondent distinction.

Four experimental projects in the book suggest applications of the theory and some of its everyday relevance. This is by no means a book of applied psychology; neither is it an account of a dead theory.

The material in this book has been student-tested and revised a number of times. A teachers' manual will be available (see the Appendix: Prepublication Research and Revisions, the section entitled "Further Validation").

1 Conditioning: a theory of learning in terms of stimulus, response, and association, *The Psychology of Learning, Yearbook XLI, Part II* (Chicago: National Society for the Study of Education, 1942), p. 18.

Chirapa Boonypisit, C. B. Ferster, George L. Geis, John B. Gilpin, James G. Holland, Joseph Mayer, M. R. Nigro, Douglas Porter, Evalyn Segal, and Virginia Voeks are among those who have given me critical guidance at various stages. I owe much to them and to others who have read different forms of one or more of these lessons as the lessons developed. Even more I owe thanks to the students who have gradually shaped my behavior.

To the Student

There are many items in these lessons. Most items consist of a brief discussion with certain words or phrases omitted. Omissions are indicated by numbered spaces: (1)______________. *Usually* (*but not always*) only one word is omitted. (*Sometimes* an entire phrase or sentence is omitted.) In the blank spaces, on an answer sheet, or in your notebook, write out the word or words that you feel belong in each blank space. Complete each item immediately after you read the item. *Use a piece of paper or cardboard to cover the items that you have not yet answered.*

Unfortunately, completing the items without thinking about them is not enough. Activity does not guarantee learning:

> The psychologist E. C. Stanford once wrote that he read in his family the form of Morning Prayer of the Episcopal Church no less than five thousand times in the course of twenty-five years, yet that he was unable to recall the prayers unaided.
>
> —JOHN FREDERICK DASHIELL[2]

At the end of each lesson you will find a brief list of questions concerning the *main* points covered in the lesson. The lesson may or may not have prepared you sufficiently so that you can answer all of these questions easily, but it will have given you a good foundation for understanding the questions. A student should not go on to a more ad-

2 *Fundamentals of General Psychology* (Boston: Houghton Mifflin, 1949), p. 372.

vanced lesson until he can answer perfectly on a test all of the end-of-chapter questions for the previous lessons.

Try to do an entire lesson at one time. Try not to do more than one lesson at one time. This will take some planning. In order to help you, a time estimate is given for each lesson (except for the projects). About half of the author's students found that they required more time than the time estimate and about half found that they needed less time. The time estimate for the entire book (exclusive of the projects) is six and one-half hours. Many students can do these lessons in less than the estimated time. However, experiments with programmed materials (G. L. Groper and G. D. Kress, Jr. Nonadaptive consequences of self-pacing in programed instruction. *NSPI Journal* [1966], 5:14–15) show that *for students with the same IQs those who spend the least time on a programmed lesson tend to learn the least.*

Major Concepts

Lesson 1

STIMULUS-ACTION. A stimulus-action upon an individual *is an event that is eliciting or changing a response* by that individual.

PROPER STIMULUS. A proper stimulus *for an individual is any event that* is able to *elicit or change a response from that individual (whether the event is a stimulus-action at that time or not).*

Lesson 2

EXPERIMENTERS' STIMULUS. *An* experimenters' stimulus *is any* event or agent *that an experimenter* can measure.

COGNITIVE STIMULUS. A cognitive stimulus *is an* event or agent *to which a person* says *he is responding.*

Lesson 3

BEHAVIORAL SITUATION. *The* behavioral situation *of an individual consists of all of the stimulus-actions upon him at that certain time.*

PHYSICAL SITUATION. *The* physical situation *of an individual consists of all experimenters' stimuli which are around that individual at that time.*

Lesson 4

RESPONDENT (a) A response for which there is at least one specific unconditioned stimulus.
(b) A response that consists of the same kind of change in the individual each time it happens.

OPERANT (a) A response for which there is no unconditioned stimulus.

(b) A response that is named and identified according to the effect it has rather than according to how it is done (can usually be done in several different ways).

Lesson 5

RESPONDENT CONDITIONING. Respondent conditioning *is the name for the process by which a stimulus-action becomes conditioned to elicit a respondent by being associated* with that respondent.

UNCONDITIONED STIMULUS-ACTION (abbreviated UCS). *An* unconditioned *stimulus-action for a respondent is a stimulus-action that will elicit that respondent without any conditioning being needed.*

CONDITIONED STIMULUS-ACTION (abbreviated CS). *A conditioned stimulus-action for a respondent is a stimulus-action that would not normally elicit that respondent before respondent conditioning but does elicit it after conditioning.*

Lesson 7

OPERANT CONDITIONING. Operant conditioning *is the name for the process by which a behavioral situation comes to produce a certain type of operant by the individual more and more frequently when such operants are followed by reinforcing consequences.*

DISCRIMINATIVE STIMULUS (abbreviated S^D). A discriminative *stimulus is a stimulus that indicates to the individual what operants will bring about what events in this situation.*

REINFORCING CONSEQUENCE. A reinforcing consequence *of an operant is an event that happens after the operant and increases the probability that this type of* of *operant will be repeated in future similar situations.*

Lesson 9

OPERANT SHAPING. Operant shaping *is the development of new operant-sequences as a result of interaction of a particular kind of individual with a particular kind of environment.*

Lesson 10

PRINCIPLE A: RESPONDENT CONDITIONING. *Conditioning requires only* one *association. Every stimulus-action immediately and completely becomes* CS *for* all *of the respondents elicited from the individual by the other stimulus-actions in the behavioral situation at that time.*

PRINCIPLE B: DYNAMIC SITUATIONS. *An individual is not likely ever to be in exactly the same total behavioral situation twice in his life.*

PRINCIPLE C: RESPONSE PROBABILITY. *When there is no* UCS *acting to elicit or to stop the respondent, the more stimulus-actions in the behavioral situation at that time that are* CS *for that respondent, the more likely the behavioral situation will elicit that respondent from the individual.*

Lesson 11

PRINCIPLE D: CONDITIONED STIMULI. *The conditioned stimulus-action usually is a group or pattern of several proper stimuli.*

PRINCIPLE E: PERMANENCY OF CONDITIONING. *Conditioning is permanent. The only way that* CS *for a respondent can stop being* CS *for that respondent is by conditioning* CS *to an incompatible respondent.*

RESPONDENT EXTINCTION. Respondent extinction *is the name of the process by which* CS *for a respondent stops being* CS *for that respondent by being associated with situations in which the respondent is not elicited (that is, by occurring in situations without* UCS).

Lesson 12

PRINCIPLE F: CONTIGUITY AND OPERANTS. *Any specific operant can be analyzed into a sequence of muscular contractions. Each of these muscular contractions is respondent. Therefore, Principle A can be applied to operants.*

PRINCIPLE G: INTENSITY OF RESPONSE. *When a response is intense, the behavioral situation of the individual is constricted. More muscles and glands participate in the total response and fewer unrelated responses occur.*

LESSON 13

REINFORCEMENT. Reinforcement *is the process involved when a reinforcer provides a reinforcing consequence.*

PUNISHMENT. Punishment *is the process involved when the onset of a negative reinforcer or the termination of a positive reinforcer follows a response.*

Important derivations and explanations:

1. Relationship between operants and respondents, pp. 127–134.
2. Explanation for response extinction, pp. 160–162.
3. Explanation for apparent gradualness of the process of conditioning, pp. 166–169.
4. Explanation for the operation of reinforcement, pp. 177–180.

PART I

Stimulus and Response

LESSON

1

Stimulus-Action

[Estimated time: 35 minutes]

> . . . In each adjustment there is always both a *response* or *act* and a *stimulus* or *situation* which call out the response. Without going too far beyond our facts, it seems possible to say that the stimulus is always provided by the environment, external to the body, or by the movements of man's own muscles and the secretions of his glands: finally, that the responses always follow relatively immediately upon the presentation or incidence of the stimulus. These are really assumptions, but they seem to be basal ones for psychology.
>
> —JOHN B. WATSON[1]

Carefully read the statement given above about stimuli and responses. Watson says that those who study psychology start from certain basal (1) __________.

The assumptions of a scientific theory or system are not a religious creed, nor are they a statement of faith (though a man may take them as his creed or faith). These assumptions do not deny the possibility and they do not deny the importance of other approaches.

1 *Psychology from the Standpoint of a Behaviorist* (Philadelphia: Lippincott, 1919), p. 10.

Early behaviorism and modern behavioral psychology do not assume any "mind" inside the organism that consciously controls its (2)__________.

We shall study behavior and specific responses in this book. We shall not study the mind in this book, *nor shall we study the brain*. We shall try to limit our terminology and frame of reference primarily to description of *behavior* of intact and complete organisms, and the *stimuli and conditions that affect this* (3)__________.

An experimental analysis is not of great value unless the observations are carefully done and carefully (4)__________ in a report for others to read.

The descriptions we write must be accurate. I may very much disagree with someone else's theoretical position *but still read his experimental reports*. I may then formulate my own theory to account for his results. I can do this only if I know the precise meaning of his descriptive terms, only if we "speak the same (5)__________" (to use a popular phrase).

In the natural sciences, we find it better to base as many of our definitions as possible upon direct observation and concrete examples. This gives natural science a very strong foundation for its handling of certain kinds of problems (and makes it nonsense for natural science to try to handle certain other kinds of problems).

EMPIRICAL DEFINITIONS

To define a word is to tell what the word means. One way to define a word is to point to an example. For instance, one way to define the word "chair" is to say "chair" and point your finger at a (6)____________.

Some words can not be clearly defined by pointing. We can point to a chair but we can not (7)____________ to a thought or a feeling.

We can point to a girl who is crying and say: "She is feeling sad." But the girl may be crying because she is very very happy. Crying may come from the smell of pepper or from being very very happy. Every person who cries is not necessarily feeling (8)____________.

To take another example, in an experiment in psychology if we say that the dog subject was "very hungry," can another person tell exactly how hungry our dog was, or *exactly* what we mean? (9)____________. (*yes* or *no*?)

Instead of saying that the dog was "very hungry" we might say: "The dog was fed for thirty minutes each day until two days before the experiment started. Then for forty-eight hours the dog was not given anything to (10)____________."

When we say when and how much the dog ate, we are much clearer and more exact when we say the dog was (11) "______."

"Hungry" and "sad" are words that refer to feelings. In this book we shall study more about behavior than about thoughts and feelings.

Definitions based on pointing or describing, definitions that tell us where to look or what to do, are called "empirical (12)______."

Empirical definitions are definitions based on pointing or describing, definitions that tell us where to look or what to do. We shall try to give an (13)______ definition for each important word or term used in this book.

STIMULUS AND RESPONSE

Before we study the empirical definitions for "stimulus" and "response," let us consider their simplest dictionary definitions. These two words are words taken into English from Latin. "Goad" and "spur" are synonyms for the word "stimulus." "Answer" and "reply" are synonyms for the word (14) "______."

When we say that "answer" and "reply" are synonyms for the word "response," we mean that "answer" and "reply" have the same or nearly the same meaning as (15)"__________."

Response means any change in an individual that is an (16)__________, or reply, to a stimulus.

In the quotation at the beginning of this lesson, Watson says that every (17)__________ (*response* or *stimulus*?) is called out by some (18)__________ (*response* or *stimulus*?).

Most psychologists assume that every response, everything that an individual does, is dependent upon some stimulus. Thus, "stimulus" is a very basic term in the science of psychology. It is important to study its exact empirical meaning. In these lessons, you will learn definitions for *four* different usages of the term "stimulus." We shall study two of these definitions in this lesson.

When we refer to *more than one* stimulus we use the plural form, which is "stimuli." Thus we say "two (19)__________," not "two stimulus."

STIMULUS–ACTION

In order to clarify the precise ways in which the term "stimulus" is used, let us first of all take an example from physiology:

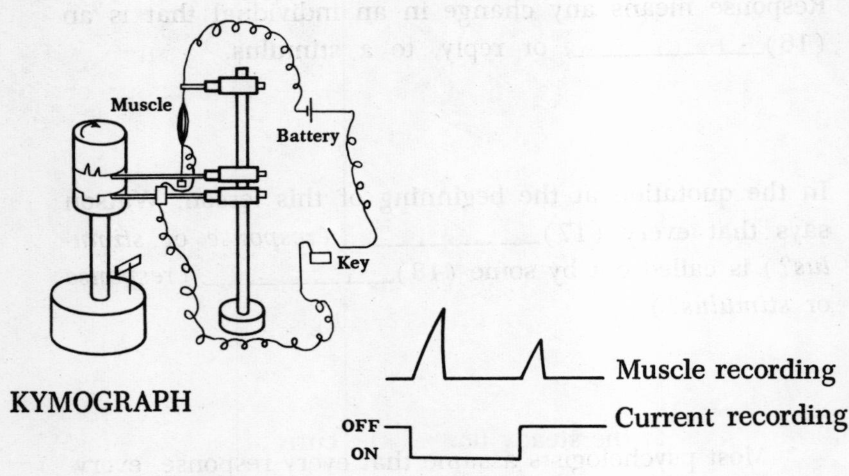

Kymograph Recording of a *make twitch* and a *break twitch.*

We arrange a muscle-nerve preparation so that movement of the muscle will be recorded. Then we stimulate the muscle by means of current from a battery. When the current enters the muscle we see a movement of the muscle. We call such a single movement a *twitch.* When we break the current we see another twitch. The recording shows that *during* the steady flow of the current the muscle returns to normal.

In this example, the current from the battery was the (20)__________, and the twitch of the muscle was the (21)__________.

But there were (22)__________ (*one* or *two*?) twitches.

There were *two* twitches! The first twitch response was elicited by the *onset* (the beginning) of the current. The second twitch response was elicited by the *termination* of the (23)__________.

The onset of the current and the termination of the current *both* elicited responses. During the steady flow of the current the muscle returned to (24)__________.

It appears that the steady flow of the current did not elicit any (25)__________.

The steady *flow* of the current *did not* elicit any twitch response. The twitches were elicited by the (26)__________ of the current and by the (27)__________ of the current, *not* by the flow of the current.

The onset and the termination of a current are *events* that elicit twitches. The flow of the current is the *agent* that provides these (28)__________ that elicit twitches.

An event that elicits a response from an organism is called a (29)____________ (*stimulus* or *response*?).

The steadily flowing current *is not* an event and *does not* elicit any response. *Changes* in current flow *are events* that *can* stimulate. For example, termination of the current acts as a stimulus. This *change* in the current is an (30)____________ (*agent* or *event*?).

The change in current is an event. The current itself is an (31)____________ to which or by which these events happen.

The steady flow of the electric current is an agent. It appears that there must be some event, some change in the stimulus-agent or in the relationship to the stimulus-agent, if there is going to be a (32)____________.

It was the onset and the termination of the current that (33)____________ed responses.

Any event that *elicits* a response is a *stimulus-action*. Any event that *changes* a response is also a "*stimulus-* (34)____________."

A stimulus-action is any (35)____________ that is *eliciting or changing* a response.

A stimulus-action is any event that is eliciting or (36)____________ a (37)____________.

DEFINITION: A stimulus-action *is an event that is eliciting or changing a response.*

PROPER STIMULI

It might be better if the word "stimulus" always meant "stimulus-action." Unfortunately this is not the case. The word "stimulus" is used in several different ways: Events that are not stimulus-actions are often called "stimuli"; agents such as the steady flow of electric current are also commonly called "stimuli."

An event that *does* elicit or change a response from an individual is called a stimulus-(38)____________ *upon* that individual.

A broader classification of stimuli would include events that are *able* to (39)____________ or change a response *whether they are stimulus-actions upon the individual at that time or not.*

DEFINITION: A proper stimulus *for an individual is any event that* is able to *elicit or change a response from that individual (whether the event is a stimulus-action at that time or not).*

Both stimulus-actions and proper stimuli are always events. The difference is that a stimulus-action is an event that (40)____________ (*does* or *is able to*?) elicit or change a response, whereas a proper stimulus for the individual is an event that (41)____________ (*does* or *is able to*?) elicit or change a response.

A *stimulus-action does*; a *proper stimulus is able to*. Thus all stimulus-actions are proper stimuli, but all proper stimuli present for an individual are not necessarily stimulus-actions upon him. Most of the proper stimuli for an individual at any time are merely *potential* stimuli (they could affect him but are not affecting him).

SOME EXAMPLES

If a boy takes a girl to a dance who has exactly the same acuity of eyesight and hearing that he has, all of the same events will be (42)____________ (*stimulus-actions* or *proper stimuli*?) for both of them.

The same events will be proper stimuli for both of them, but the girl may notice the exact color and style of other girls' dresses where the boy may not pay any attention at all to such details. In this case the details of the girls' dresses are stimulus-(43)____________ upon the girl but not upon the boy.

The stimulus-actions upon an individual are always only a small part of the proper stimuli around him at that time.

To give another example, many teachers find that if they ask a question of a class in general and then call on a specific student to answer, the student often will not be able to answer unless the question is repeated. The words the teacher spoke the first time were not stimulus-actions upon all of the students, although they were (44)__________ stimuli for all of them.

There is a proper stimulus in this lesson that is sometimes not a stimulus-action: the sight of the quotation at the beginning of the lesson. Some students incorrectly answer item one with the word "stimulus" or the word "response." The only possible explanation for this would seem to be that they did not read the quotation, or read only the first part of it. No student can learn anything from a lesson or any part of a lesson that he does not read. You can not learn even from a proper stimulus if it is not a (45)__________ upon you.

REVIEW

Stimulus-actions upon an individual are always stimulus (46)__________ (*agents* or *events*?).

However, all stimulus-events do not make the individual respond. Stimulus-events that do not make the individual respond are not stimulus-(47)__________ (*actions* or *agents*?) upon that individual.

A *stimulus-action* is an *event* that (48)__________ (*does* or *is able to*?) make the individual respond.

A stimulus-action is an event that does make an individual respond.

A *proper stimulus* is an event that (49)__________ (*does* or *is able to*?) make that individual respond.

A stimulus-action is an (50)__________ that *is making* the individual respond.

Responses are elicited or changed by *events* such as changes in stimulus-agents, changes in grouping or patterns of stimulus-agents, changes in the individual, and changes in the relationship between these factors. When events do elicit or change responses, they are called stimulus-(51)__________ (*actions* or *agents*?).

Both stimulus-actions and potential stimuli are (52)__________ stimuli.

SELF-TEST: Take the following self-test. Then carefully correct your mistakes or omissions. Do not study Lesson 2 until you know that you can answer the test questions for Lesson 1 without any mistakes or omissions. *Follow this policy for every lesson in this book and you will gain greater understanding with less expenditure of time and effort.*

LESSON TEST: AFTER YOU HAVE COMPLETED THIS LESSON, ANSWER THE FOLLOWING QUESTIONS WITHOUT LOOKING BACK AT THE LESSON:

1. According to the quotation at the beginning of this lesson, psychology starts from certain basal _________ (*assumptions* or *beliefs*?) about _____________ (*mind*, *brain*, or *behavior*?)

2. Define "stimulus-action."

3. Define "proper stimulus."

4. Pick some game or sport and give an example of some kind of event that happens fairly often in this sport that might be a proper stimulus for both of two individuals but is likely, most of the time, to be a stimulus-action (i.e., "to be noticed") only by one who knows the sport well.

CHECK YOUR ANSWERS (OR, MUCH BETTER, EXCHANGE ANSWERS WITH SOMEONE ELSE AND CHECK EACH OTHER'S ANSWERS) BY LOOKING BACK AT THE LESSON. CAREFULLY CORRECT EVERY MISTAKE OR OMISSION.

NOTES:

1. One type of empirical definition is called "operational definition." Some scholars might say that these two terms may be used interchangeably. The expression "empirical definition" is more general and more descriptive of the definitions in this book.

[16]

2. J. J. Gibson (The concept of stimulus in psychology, *Amer. Psychologist*, [1960] *15*:694–703) has published a somewhat different and more technical discussion of the term "stimulus" than we undertake in this book. Advanced students should examine Gibson's article.

LESSON

2

Experimenters' Stimuli

[Estimated time: 25 minutes]

. . . The hour that you spend in the waiting-room of a village station and the hour that you spend in watching an amusing play are physically equal; they measure alike in units of 1 sec. To you, the one hour goes slowly, the other quickly; they are not equal. Take two circular boxes of different diameter (say, 2 cm and 8 cm), and pour sand into them until they both weigh, say 50 gr. The two masses are physically equal; placed on the pans of a balance, they will hold the beam level. To you, as you lift them in your hands, or raise them in turn by the same hand, the box of smaller diameter is considerably the heavier.

—EDWARD BRADFORD TITCHENER[1]

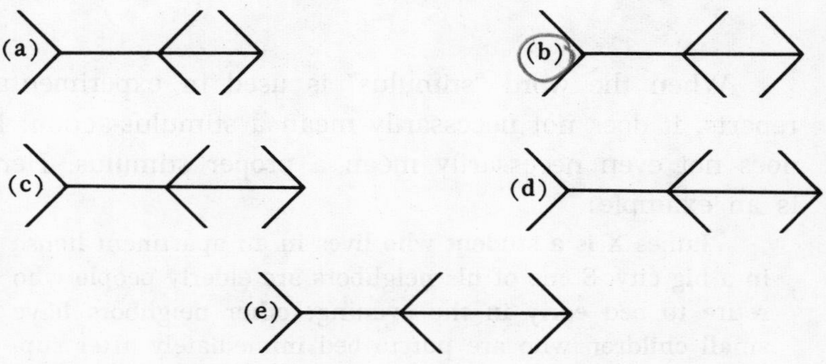

1. Which horizontal line is divided into two equal parts? *Choose, then measure.* Have one or two other people try it also.

1 *Textbook of Psychology* (New York: Macmillan, 1910), p. 7.

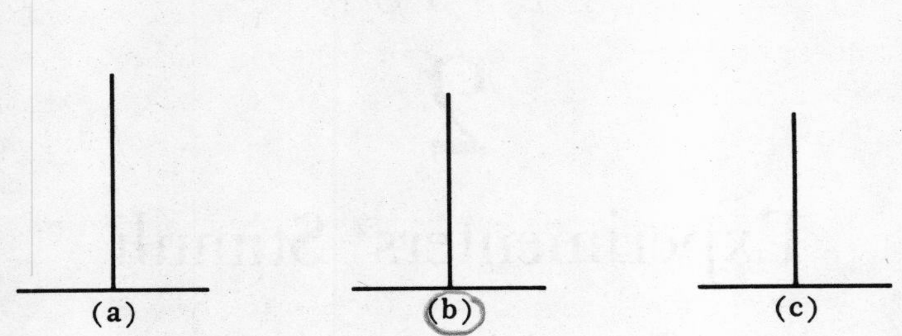

2. In which case is the horizontal line equal in length to the vertical line? Choose, then measure. Have one or two other people try it also.

EXPERIMENTERS' STIMULI

A *proper stimulus* is an event that (3)________ (*does* or *is able to*?) elicit or change a response by that individual.

An event that *does* elicit or change a response is a (4)________.

When the word "stimulus" is used in experimental reports, it does not necessarily mean a stimulus-action. It does not even necessarily mean a proper stimulus. Here is an example:

> James X is a student who lives in an apartment house in a big city. Some of his neighbors are elderly people who retire to bed early in the evening; other neighbors have small children who are put to bed immediately after supper. Jim has a pet dog that he has trained to stay around the building and away from the streets. The neighbors have complained about the noise Jim makes when he whistles for his dog to come in each evening.

One of Jim's friends at school told him about a high frequency whistle that a dog can hear but human beings can not hear at all. Jim decided to try out such whistles. As he did not know how high a frequency either human beings or dogs could hear (and, let us assume, he could not find a book with this information), he made two whistles that neither he nor his friends could hear. He tested the whistles and learned the actual frequency of the noise of each. Then he tried them out with his dog. He was able to teach the dog to come in when whistle number two was blown but the dog paid no attention at all to whistle number one (which had a much higher frequency than number two).

In this investigation James X used the sounds of the whistles as stimuli. Blowing whistle number (5)_______ turned out to be a satisfactory way to call the dog.

The sounds of both whistles would ordinarily be called "stimuli used in this study" in a report by James X, even though James could not (6)__________ either of the sounds and the dog responded to only one of them.

Whistle number one was not a proper stimulus for either James X or the dog. Whistle number two was not a proper stimulus for James X. Yet James X could measure both sounds by means of an oscilloscope and he would call them both "stimuli." Thus we need a third definition for the word (7)______________.

DEFINITION: *An* experimenters' stimulus *is any* event or agent *that an experimenter* can measure.

COGNITIVE STIMULI

"To see is to believe!" Some say that if we see something with our own (8)____________, it must be true.

In the examples at the beginning of this lesson we showed that measurements with a rule sometimes do not agree with what our eyes seem to (9)____________.

A dog seems to see things differently from the way an elephant sees them. One person, furthermore, will sometimes see things (10)____________ from the way another person sees them.

Many experiments in psychology analyze the relationship between (a) *what people say* that they see, or hear, or feel, and (b) *measurements* of (11)____________ (*experimenters' stimuli* or *proper stimuli*?).

As we demonstrated in the examples at the beginning of this lesson, a visual stimulus as a person knows it by measurement (which we call an "experimenters' stimulus") is sometimes not the same as the stimulus as a person says that he sees it.

We shall call a stimulus as a person *says* that he sees it a cognitive (12)______________.

DEFINITION: *A* cognitive stimulus *is an* event or agent *to which a person* says *he is responding.*

If we define the cognitive stimuli for a person according to what the person says, an important question might be: "If a person *does not say anything*, is he still responding to (13)______________ stimuli?"

No one else can tell for certain whether events or agents are cognitive stimuli to a person if he does not (14)__________ anything.

What a person says shows what events or agents are (15)______________ stimuli to him.

At one time, cognitive stimuli were the main things studied by psychologists. In a psychological experiment, the experimenter would present some stimulus and the person being studied (the subject) would respond by (16)______________ing what he saw, or heard, or felt.

Saying or telling what you see, or hear, or feel (talking about your cognitive stimuli) is called "introspection." The word "introspection" comes from Latin *intro-* meaning "within" and *specere* meaning "to look." To "introspect" means to (17)______________ within oneself.

I can "look within" myself. I can tell you what I see or hear. I can also tell you what I think or feel. You can

not "look within" me and tell what I see, or hear, or think, or feel. You can only observe my behavior and listen to what I (18)______________ to you when I introspect.

Because cognitive stimuli are what the *subject* (the individual being studied) says he is responding to, cognitive stimuli are called (19)______________ (*objective* or *subjective*?).

Cognitive stimuli are called "subjective" because they are the events and agents to which the (20)____________ (*experimenter* or *subject*?) says he is responding.

Experimenters' stimuli are events and agents that the experimenter can (21)______________ (*control* or *measure*?).

The agents that the experimenter measures are often *objects* (such as the lines in the examples at the beginning of this lesson). Experimenters' stimuli are called (22)______________ (*objective* or *subjective*?).

Experimenters' stimuli are usually called "objective." Cognitive stimuli are usually called "subjective."

Philosophers have long been concerned about the relationship between cognitive stimuli and experimenters' stimuli. For example, some philosophers (*Idealists*) might say that *experimenters' stimuli are not ultimately real*, that reality is essentially mental or spiritual, that experimenters' stimuli are merely one kind of cognitive stimuli. Other philosophers (*Materialists*) might say that *only experimenters' stimuli are ultimately real*, that all science is essentially reducible to physics, that so-called "thinking" or "cognition" is merely subvocal speech or implicit action.

REVIEW

a. All events that an experimenter (such as James X) uses as stimuli in an experiment (28)____________ (*are* or *are not*?) necessarily eliciting or changing responses.

b. Events that are not stimulus-actions upon an individual may still be (24)______________ stimuli for him (and may be experimenters' stimuli used by an experimenter studying him).

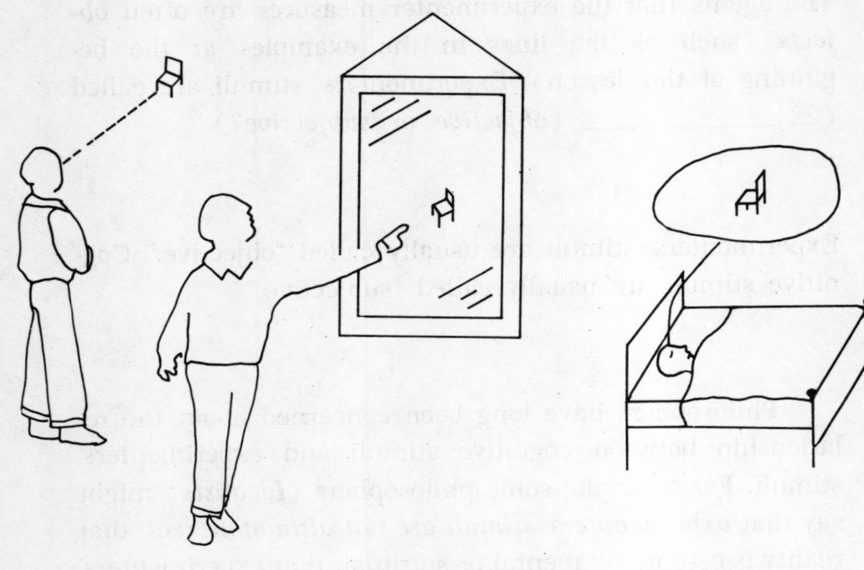

What is 'real"?

Do they all "see" the same girl?

c. Every event around an individual that is a proper stimulus for him is not necessarily a (25)________ upon him.

d. All stimulus-actions must also be (26)________ (*cognitive stimuli* or *proper stimuli*?).

e. We are often affected by events that we do not "consciously" notice at the time. Such events are not cognitive stimuli to us but they are (27)________.

f. Stimulus-actions are always proper stimuli. Events that are not cognitive stimuli, not stimulus-actions, and not even proper stimuli may still be tried as (28)________ stimuli in an experiment.

g. An experimenters' stimulus is any event *or agent* that an experimenter can (29)________.

h. Because they can be measured, we call experimenters' stimuli (30)________ (*objective* or *subjective*?).

i. Agents may be cognitive stimuli or experimenters' stimuli, *but only events* (changes in the agent or in the relationship between the agent and the individual) are (31)________ upon an individual or (32)________ for him.

j. Events, not agents, are stimulus-actions or proper stimuli. An event that does elicit or change a response by the individual is a (33)______________.

k. An event that is able (whether it does or not) to elicit or change a response by an individual is a (34)______________.

l. An event or agent that an individual says he is responding to is a (35)______________.

Most of the experiments done by psychologists until after 1900 concerned the study of cognitive stimuli in comparison to experimenters' stimuli. Experimental psychophysics is still a major area of both "pure" and "applied" research. The results of these experiments have many applications and implications for such widely varying areas as advertising, courtroom testimony, equipment design, education, instrument panel design, interior decorating, propaganda, theater. One of the great American psychologists who studied such relationships was Edward Bradford Titchener. The quotation at the beginning of this lesson is from one of his books. Modern psychophysical experiments are not limited to the study of cognitive stimuli. Instead of requiring an individual to say what he sees or hears, he may respond in some other way (e.g., by pressing a certain lever). Thus modern psychophysics studies all sorts of stimulus-action, not just cognitive stimuli.

LESSON TEST: AFTER YOU HAVE COMPLETED THIS LESSON, ANSWER THE FOLLOWING QUESTIONS WITHOUT LOOKING BACK AT THE LESSON:

1. Why are cognitive stimuli called "subjective"?
2. Define "cognitive stimulus."
3. Define "stimulus-action."
4. Define "proper stimulus."
5. Define "experimenters' stimulus."
6. Look back at the brief discussion (just before the review) of materialism and idealism. A scientist may be an idealist or he may be a materialist. (These two, of course, are not the only possibilities.) Regardless of his personal belief or faith, in his work and in his writings about his work a scientist usually seems to others to be a materialist.
   a. What is it about scientific reports that makes it seem that scientists are materalists?
   b. Many scientists are idealists. How is this possible?

CHECK YOUR ANSWERS (OR EXCHANGE ANSWERS AND CHECK) BY LOOKING BACK AT THE LESSON. CAREFULLY CORRECT EVERY MISTAKE OR OMISSION.

LESSON 3

Situations

[Estimated time: 35 minutes]

It will probably be clear from the earlier discussion of objects that the "environment" means the psychological environment, *i.e.*, the environment *as it is for the behaving person.* This is sometimes sufficiently like the objective (physical or social or conceptual) environment so that description in terms of the latter will convey the psychological reality. But more often this is not possible. A ten-foot board fence may be a barrier to me, if I want something on the other side, but not to a crow, a caterpillar, an elephant, or a good pole vaulter. And it is exactly or chiefly its barrierness that is psychologically relevant and behavior determining.

—D. K. Adams[1]

A response is an answer or reply to some (1)____________.

Because a response is an answer or reply to some stimulus, we *might* say that the stimulus-action causes the (2)____________.

1 *The Anatomy of Personality* (Garden City, N.Y.: Doubleday, 1954), p. 9.

When we say "The stimulus *causes* the response," however, this seems to suggest that the stimulus, by itself, is the total or whole (3)______________ of the response.

No one stimulus-action, by itself, is the total cause of a (4)______________.

An action by some stimulus seems to be necessary for any response (even every individual movement or twitch of a muscle). Even the simplest twitch, however, is *caused* by a total *situation*, *not* by just one (5)______________.

Not just one stimulus-action, but the stimulus-action as a part of a total (6)______________ is the cause of a response.

The total situation determines the response to a particular (7)______________.

For example, ordinarily an animal will move when it is hit by a pointed stick. However, a completely tired (exhausted) (8)______________ will not move.

If the animal is completely exhausted, the action by the stick may be the same, but the *total* (whole) (9)______________ of the animal is different.

An individual may make *Response A* (move away) in most situations when *Stimulus A* (being hit with a stick) occurs. When *Stimulus B* (the whole group of internal stimulus-events from being very tired) occurs, usually the animal may make *Response B* (lie down). When *Stimulus A* and *Stimulus B* occur together, there is a completely different situation. In this (10)____________ the animal may not make *Response A*.

In a total situation containing *Stimulus A* and *Stimulus B* the animal may not make *Response A* and he may not make *Response B*. He may make a completely different response: *Response C* (stand still).

THE BEHAVIORAL SITUATION

Every stimulus-action upon an individual is a part of the *total* (11)____________ to which he is responding.

All of the stimulus-actions upon an individual in combination (grouping and joining) make his (12)__________ (*behavioral situation* or *physical situation*, which would you call it?).

We shall say that the total *behavioral* situation of an individual at a certain time includes (consists of) all of the stimulus-(13)____________ upon him.

Proper stimuli for an individual that are not affecting him (i.e., potential stimuli) at the time (14)__________ (*are* or *are not*?) part of his behavioral situation.

Proper stimuli for an individual that are not affecting him at at the time (i.e., potential stimuli:) *are not* part of his (15)__________ situation.

The total behavioral situation includes (consists of) only those events that *do* affect the individual at that certain (16)__________.

DEFINITION: *The* behavioral situation *of an individual consists of all of the stimulus-actions upon him at that certain time.*

THE PHYSICAL SITUATION

The behavioral situation includes every (17)__________ (*event* or *agent*?) that *does* produce or change some response.

An individual does not respond to every event to which he could respond. Only those events that are affecting an individual at that time are in his behavioral situation. A human being, furthermore, can not respond without instruments to every event that he can measure with instruments. Many of the events that an experimenter can measure are never, by themselves, stimulus-(18)actions upon any human being.

Stimulus-actions upon an experimenter are events to which the experimenter does respond directly. *Experimenters' stimuli* are stimuli that the experimenter *can measure* whether or not he can or does ever (19)__________ to them directly himself.

Many events are always present to which no human being can or does respond directly, but which human experimenters can measure. Events that are experimenters' stimuli are *not* necessarily stimulus-(20)__________ upon the experimenter.

Stimulus-actions upon the experimenter are *events* to which he is responding directly. Experimenters' stimuli are *events* and *agents* that the experimenter in some way can (21)__________.

The most basic science concerned with measurement is the science of physics. We call the total of all experimenters' stimuli that are around an individual the (22)__________ (*physical* or *physiological*?) situation of that individual.

DEFINITION: *The* physical situation *of an individual consists of all experimenters' stimuli which are around that individual at that time.*

BEHAVIORAL SITUATION, SET, AND HABIT

When we say that we *set* a table in a particular place, we mean that we *put* the table in that place. But the word "set" also has other meanings. We may (23)"________ a table" without moving the table.

When we *set* a table without moving it, we *prepare* the table for something. (For example, we may set the table for dinner, or for tea, or for card playing.) "To set" may mean "to put" and it may mean to (24)"________ for something."

When we *prepare* for something, we "get *set*" for it. For example, we may "get set" for a race, for an examination, for a fight, or for a good time at a party.

A person changes his physical situation when he (25)________s a table to prepare it for dinner.

When a person *sets a table*, he changes his physical situation. However, a person can *get set for a good time* at a party without changing his (26)________ situation at all.

A person can get set for a good time at a party *without preparing or changing his physical situation*. For example, a person can get set for a good time at a party by preparing to act in a certain way, that is, by preparing his (27)____________ situation without changing his physical situation at all.

A person's behavioral situation depends in part upon his *set* (his behavioral preparation). If I tell you to listen for the sound of running water, you are very likely to hear the (28)____________ of running water much sooner than someone who is not listening for it.

What sounds or noises a person is *able* to hear are *limited* to the proper stimuli for him which occur. Which proper stimuli he *will* hear depends in part on his *set*, such as being told to listen for something.

Set is not necessarily temporary. For example:

> The mother of a small baby is entertaining evening guests in her living room. In the midst of a relatively noisy general conversation the baby, in a room above, begins to cry. The mother promptly excuses herself and disappears upstairs, whereupon it turns out that no one else had even heard the baby. For her to be able to react selectively in this way, it is not at all necessary that her hearing be superior to that of her husband or her guests. Neither need her attention have been divided before the crying started, for she can react just as effectively right out of a

sound sleep, even though her husband neither stirs at the time nor recalls a disturbance in the morning.

—NORMAN CAMERON[2]

In this example, some of the people at the party have better hearing than others. However, the (29)__________ (*behavioral* or *physical*) situation in the room is almost exactly the same for everyone.

The general physical situation in the room is almost exactly the same for everyone. The mother and a young lady in the room might have equally good ears; yet the mother would hear the baby when the young lady did not. This means that the (30)__________ (*behavioral* or *physical?*) situation of the mother is different from that of the young lady.

The mother's set is quite different from the set of the young lady. The mother's baby asleep upstairs and the many times the mother has responded to the cries of the baby *have prepared the mother to respond more quickly and sensitively to the baby.* The mother's behavioral situation is different from that of the young lady. This is because the mother's *preparation* or (31)__________ is different.

The mother's set is different from the set of the young lady. Psychologists have found that not only our set from

2 *The Psychology of Behavior Disorders* (Boston: Houghton Miffin, 1947), p. 67.

something that has recently happened (such as being told something or having a baby and putting it to bed nearby) but our whole lifelong history of past responses (our *reactional biography*) influences what events will be stimulus-actions. For example:

> The clear superiority in visual perception that an experienced sailor shows at sea . . . used to be . . . held to mean superior optic sensitivity, and few doubted that slender hypersensitive fingers were basic equipment for skillful surgery.
>
> . . . Under the uniform conditions of an eye clinic or a psychological laboratory, any number of landlubbers can be found who test higher in visual acuity than the average seaman, even though they are unquestionably inferior to him in detecting a landfall or ships on the horizon. As for surgery, some of the world's most proficient and eminent operators have short stubby fingers and yet, though wearing rubber gloves, they can still feel things that the most slender-fingered layman could not detect with his bare hands.
>
> . . . two men with different habits may enter an objectively identical situation and react oppositely. Or one man may give a prompt reaction because he has acquired special behavior in previous similar situations, and another give no specific appropriate reactions because he has no reaction ready which the situation can elicit.
>
> —Norman Cameron[3]

These examples show that both temporary (32)____________, as in the case of the mother, and long-time habit, (33)____________ (*reactional biography* or *set*?) may account for different responses by different individuals to similar physical situations.

[3] *Op. cit.*, pp. 65 ff.

THE "SAME" ENVIRONMENT

Brothers have the same parents; but they may have hair of different kinds or colors, different heights, and all kinds of other differences. Two brothers usually (34)____________ (*do* or *do not*?) inherit *exactly* the same characteristics from their parents.

Brothers do not usually inherit exactly the same characteristics from their parents. Nor are brothers treated in exactly the same way by their parents. The parents may try to take care of each child in the same way. However, unless they are twins, one child will always have a younger brother, and the other child will have an (35)__________ brother.

Even the physical situation of a child with an older brother is not the same as the physical situation of a child who does not have an older brother. As we inherit not only characteristics such as hair color and height but sharpness of eyesight and hearing ability, the behavioral situations of two brothers are likely to be much more different than their physical situations. Only in very general terms can we accurately say that brothers have the same environment.

Two men are in exactly the same physical situation. They have exactly the same auditory acuity (hearing ability). They are spoken to in the Thai language. Both of them respond to the sounds. One of the men, however, understands only English; and the other knows only Chinese. The cognitive stimuli are the same for both men: they both hear a voice speaking in a strange (36)____________.

They are then both asked to repeat exactly what they hear. As the man who knows only Chinese knows a language similar to Thai (both Thai and Chinese are tonal languages), he responds to differences in the spoken Thai that have no effect at all upon the man who knows only (37)____________.

For the man who knows only English, the physical situation and the proper stimuli are exactly the same as for the man who knows only Chinese. Their (38)____________ situations, however, are quite different.

Differences between the behavioral situations of persons in the same physical situation may be very large. Different spoken sounds, for example, are stimulus-(39)____________ upon persons growing up where different languages are spoken.

Many Thais, for example, do not hear any difference between "hotel" and "hoten," and most Americans hear no difference between the Thai word meaning "near" and the Thai word meaning (40)"____________" (the opposite of "near").

Until a person can at least hear the difference between the words for "far" and "near," he is likely to have some real problems learning to understand much of the (41)____________ language.

Some of the Thai language is hard for an American to learn because he does not respond to the difference between certain stimuli. He is able to respond to these differences (the hearing of Americans is just as good as the hearing of Thais), but they are not stimulus-(42)____________ upon him when they occur in a spoken sentence.

Differences in stimulus-action upon two people may be the result of the kind of preparation we call (43)"____________."

Differences in stimulus-action may be the result of temporary *set*, or they may be the result of learning. As a result of set and habit, different events may be stimulus-actions for two individuals, even though the two are in *exactly* the same physical situation. Two individuals may also make different (44)____________ to exactly the same stimulus-action.

Different responses may be made by two individuals as a result of set and habit, even though all of the proper stimuli that are present for them are the same.

STIMULI AND SITUATIONS

Most psychology books give only one definition for the word "stimulus." Some psychology books define "stimulus" as "stimulus-action." Some define "stimulus" as we have defined "proper stimulus." They usually do not tell the student that the word "stimulus" may also sometimes mean what we have called a "cognitive stimulus," and may sometimes mean an (45)"____________ stimulus."

Knowing that the word "stimulus" may mean "experimenters' stimulus," "proper stimulus," "cognitive stimulus," or "stimulus-action" may help you to think more clearly and act more effectively. This is because you will know that everything that is a stimulus to you is not necessarily a (46)____________ to someone standing next to you.

Every event that is a "stimulus" to you is not necessarily a "stimulus" to someone standing next to you.

Every event in your physical situation (47)____________ (*is* or *is not*?) a part of your behavioral situation.

At any given moment most of your physical situation is not a part of your (48)______________ situation.

Your behavioral situation consists only of those events that (49)______________ (*are affecting you* or *are able to affect you*?) at that time.

Only those events that are affecting you are part of your behavioral situation and only those events around you that an experimenter can measure are part of your (50)______________ (*experimental* or *physical*?) situation.

As we have defined "physical situation," it is *not* the "total situation around you" (whatever this may really mean) but everything around you that an experimenter could (51)______________ (*control* or *measure*?).

If something cannot in any way be measured, it is not physical and not a part of an individual's physical environment. (Experimenters can and do measure many things they can not control.)

Two more situations might be defined in order to provide definitions of "situation" for all of our definitions of "stimulus." The "*physiological situation*" of an individual consists of all proper stimuli for that individual that are around that individual at that time. The "*conscious situa-*

tion" (*or "Life Space"*) of an individual consists of all cognitive stimuli for the individual at that time.

LESSON TEST: AFTER YOU HAVE COMPLETED THIS LESSON, ANSWER THE FOLLOWING QUESTIONS WITHOUT LOOKING BACK AT THE LESSON:

1. Define "behavioral situation."
2. *Most* of an individual's physical situation is not part of his behavioral situation. Define "physical situation."
3. Define "experimenters' stimulus."
4. Give an example of two individuals at a concert who are in exactly the same physical situation (*and exactly the same physiological situation*) but in quite different behavioral situations.

CHECK YOUR ANSWERS (OR EXCHANGE ANSWERS AND CHECK) BY LOOKING BACK AT THE LESSON. CAREFULLY CORRECT EVERY MISTAKE OR OMISSION.

PROJECT I

Experimental Participation in an Interpersonal Situation

. . . In general terms, behavior (B) is a function (F) of the person (P) and of his environment (E), B = F (P, E). . . .

In this formula for behavior, the state of the person (P) and that of his environment (E) are not independent of each other. How a child sees a given physical setting (for instance whether the frozen pond looks dangerous to him or not) depends upon the developmental state and the character of that child and upon his ideology. The worlds in which the newborn, the one-year-old child, and the ten-year-old child live are different even in the identical physical or social surroundings.

—KURT LEWIN[1]

Role playing provides the chance to try out new or different ways of dealing with people, without the usual risks involved on the job itself if the method fails.

. . . .

. . . In role playing, practice in listening, and in hearing what is behind the words, is as important as learning how to say your "own part." It is all part of the picture of *learning how to see the gap between your own and some-*

[1] *Field Theory and Social Science* (New York: Harper & Row, 1951), p. 239.

one else's picture of the same situation, of learning that "there's more than meets the eye" to human behavior.

—D. H. FRYER, M. R. FEINBERG, and S. S. ZALKIND[2]

It is an interesting and worthwhile experience to try to put yourself in someone else's place. This can be much easier to do than you might anticipate!

PURPOSE: To emphasize the importance of the emotional (respondent) aspects of human behavior and to concretely illustrate that two people viewing exactly the same physical situation may be in extremely different behavioral situations.

PROCEDURE: Ask someone to cooperate with you on this project. Toss a coin in order to decide who plays role A first and who plays role B first. Carefully read the description of the physical situation and the description of the behavioral situation for your role. Try to put yourself completely into the behavioral situation described. The physical situation occurred many years ago and may be quite different from any situation you have ever encountered. You will therefore have to use your imagination a little.

Part I. Play the roles for fifteen or twenty minutes. Then stop and reread the descriptions of both behavioral situations. Check to be certain that both of you have been speaking in line with the behavioral situations as described. Relax for a few minutes and do something else.

Part II. *Change* roles and put yourself into the other behavioral situation for fifteen or twenty minutes.

2 *Developing People in Industry* (New York: Harper & Row, 1956), pp. 138, 142.

PHYSICAL SITUATION

Anthracite coal mining in Eastern Pennsylvania was a sick industry even before the depression. In the 1930's still more mines shut down, the companies deciding to keep their coal in the ground until prices for it should go up. There was great unemployment and distress among the miners. In these years the unemployed miners began going into the idle mines and taking out the coal. They did this without permission of the companies which owned the mines, and without the interference of the local police, so that no violence resulted. They have both burned the coal themselves, and sold it.

—ALFRED WINSLOW JONES[3]

BEHAVIORAL SITUATION A

It is 1935. You are a miner (or a miner's wife). You (or your husband) have worked many years in the mines. You are an honest and God-fearing man and a good worker. You do not take charity from anyone. These are very hard times, but you take care of yourself and your own family. You feel that under the circumstances you have a right to use coal that you take from the mine to heat the room in which you and your family live, and also to sell it in order to be able to have some money of your own with which to care for your family. Both your minister and the police know that you and other miners are taking coal from the mines. No one has ever objected.

You are in the Post Office. You have just received a letter from a friend in Idaho who says that there are no jobs out there even if you had the money to move. You hear someone say that the miners are all thieves. When you turn to see who said it, the speaker notices you and

[3] *Life, Liberty and Property* (Philadelphia: Lippincott, 1941), p. 358.

your clothes. He (she) must know that you are a miner (or a miner's wife). You like to avoid trouble but you feel that *you must say something.*

BEHAVIORAL SITUATION B

It is 1935. You are vice-president of a coal company (or his wife). You do not own any stock in the company, but you feel a definite responsibility to the company. You feel that it is not only illegal but completely immoral for the miners to take what does not belong to them.

You are in the Post Office. You are upset about the way the Democrats have been raising taxes and putting through give-away programs. The Communists are trying to take over in Europe and Socialism is increasing in the United States. How can business get back on its feet and get us out of the depression if the government continues to raise taxes? Property rights are the basic rights on which this Republic is based. Today the government is taxing property away, and the police don't even do anything about these former mine workers stealing coal from the mines. You have just said this to a friend when you notice a miner (miner's wife) has heard you and seems to be upset by what you said.

COMMENT: The interested student or the Instructor wishing to consider this specific problem further should read Anatol Rapoport's *Strategy and Conscience* (New York: Harper & Row, 1964), particularly pp. 274–277 and the entire Part III; and Russel W. Davenport's *The Dignity of Man* (New York: Harper & Row, 1955), particularly pp. 31–40.

REPORT:

Part I. Write what happened when you tried this project.

Part II. Role playing is sometimes used by industrial and social counselors in order to help people to begin to understand each other a little better. This is why one of the quotations at the beginning of this project is from a book called *Developing People in Industry*. Describe some specific occasion in your life or in the lives of your family and close friends when practice in trying to put yourself in another person's place might have been helpful in solving some interpersonal problem or misunderstanding.

LESSON

4

Response

[Estimated time: 25 minutes]

Before talking about principles, a line must be drawn between two kinds of behavior. One kind has been known, since long ago, as *voluntary* behavior, and the other has usually has been called *reflex*. These two large classes of human activity together comprise just about all the examples of behavior in which a student of learning would be interested.

Voluntary and reflex, however, are bad words from the scientific point of view. The history of their use tells us they have often meant different things to different people. In fact, there has been so much disagreement about the meaning of the two words that many psychologists have recently adopted the terms *operant* and *respondent* to replace them.

—Fred S. Keller[1]

If I ask someone, "How many of the five pencils you see on the table in front of you are blue?" he probably (1)____________ (*can* or *can not*?) answer very easily.

1 *Learning: Reinforcement Theory* (Garden City, N.Y.: Doubleday, 1954), p. 20.

He can answer easily, and he can give the same answer in many ways. He can answer by pointing, by holding up a certain number of fingers, or by (2)____________ the number of pencils.

If I ask someone to make his heart beat more rapidly without moving or exercising, he probably (3)____________ (*can* or *can not*?) do this.

Most people can not make their hearts beat more rapidly. But, if something very exciting happens to a person, his heart probably will beat (4)____________ (*more rapidly* or *more slowly*?).

Heart beating more rapidly and answering a question are responses, but they are examples of very different kinds of (5)____________.

OPERANTS AND RESPONDENTS

Responses that usually can be controlled by spoken instructions or requests are called "operants." Which is operant: Answering a question, or heart beating more rapidly? (6)____________

Operants are responses that usually can be controlled by spoken instructions. Also, operants can usually be done in (7)____________ (*more than one way* or *only one way*?).

We can give the same answer to a question in more than one way. For example, we can answer the question "How many?" by speaking a number or by holding up a certain number of our (8)____________. That is, if the answer is not larger than ten!

Most adults can use their fingers or their voices to answer questions about numbers. Newborn babies (9)____________ (*can* or *can not*?) make these operants in answer to a question.

A person usually must *learn how* to make the kind of response called (10)____________ (*operant* or *respondent*?).

Before a person can make an operant such as answering a question about numbers, he must (11)____________ how to count or talk (or how to hold up only a certain number of fingers).

We do not learn how to make a respondent. For example, we (12)____________ (*do* or *do not*?) learn how to make our hearts beat.

A newborn baby's heart will beat faster when certain stimuli make the baby excited. An adult's heart beats in the same way, *but* the adult has (13)____________ed to be excited by stimuli that do not excite a newborn baby.

An adult has learned to be excited by stimuli that do not excite a newborn baby, but we do *not* learn *how* to make (14)______________ (*operants* or *respondents*?).

Excitement is respondent. We do *not learn how* to be excited; we learn *what* to be excited by. We learn to be excited by (15)______________ that do not excite a newborn baby.

We learn additional stimuli for respondents, but the *form* (the way in which the response is made) *of a respondent* usually (16)______________ (*does* or *does not*?) change during the life of an individual.

The form of a respondent usually does not change. The form of an operant usually (17)______________ (*changes* or *does not change*?) in different circumstances and as we learn to make a more and more skilled response.

The way that a three-year-old walks and talks and plays, for example, will change very much before the child is ready for first grade. By the time the child is ready for college, many of his operants will have changed in form almost as much as his physical size and appearance have changed.

DISCRIMINATIVE STIMULI AND UNCONDITIONED STIMULI

If we wish to decide whether a response is operant or respondent, we must first know whether there are stimuli that naturally (unconditionally, i.e., without learning) elicit this response. If there are such stimuli, the response is (18)____________ (*operant* or *respondent*?).

A stimulus that naturally elicits a certain respondent is called an *unconditioned* (19)____________ for that respondent.

Respondents are the kind of responses that can be elicited by *unconditione*d stimuli. Operants are the kind of responses that (20)____________ (*can* or *can not*?) be elicited by unconditioned stimuli.

An individual learns to make operants in response to *discriminative* (21)____________ that indicate what events are likely to follow what operants.

Discriminative stimuli indicate what events are likely to follow what *operants*. Discriminative stimuli indicate what the alternatives are. There are, however, no alternative *respondent* "choices." Respondents are elicited by (22)____________ (*discriminative* or *unconditioned*?) stimuli.

Answering a question is (23)__________ (*operant* or *respondent?*).

Answering a question is operant. Heart beating is (24)__________ (*operant* or *respondent?*).

For each of the following responses, tell whether you think it is *respondent* or *operant*:

Blushing (more blood than usual going to the surface of the skin and making the skin of the face change color) (25)__________

Picking up a pencil (26)__________

Solving a mathematics problem (27)__________

Sweating (28__________

Typewriting (29)__________

One can pick up a pencil, or solve a mathematics problem, or typewrite in several different ways, and there is no unconditioned stimulus for any of these responses.

"A cat that happens to jump on a hot stove lid is not likely ever to do so again. In fact, this cat may become quite emotionally upset in the future whenever it even sees a stove lid."

Jumping (whether jumping onto a stove lid or jumping about while playing) (30)__________

Becoming emotionally upset (31)__________

Running (whether running away from a stove lid or just running down a street) (32)__________

Both jumping onto a stove lid and running away from a stove lid are operant. Becoming emotionally upset is respondent.

For each of the following responses, tell whether you think that its stimuli are *discriminative* or *unconditioned*:

Driving an automobile (33)__________

Change in skin temperature (34)__________

Fear (mouth drying up, hair standing on end, and so on) (35)____________

Closing a door (36)____________

Driving an automobile and closing a door are operants and thus are guided by discriminative stimuli.

B. F. SKINNER

In 1937 B. F. Skinner published his paper first defining and discussing the technical terms "respondent" and "operant." The first definitions defined "operant" and "respondent" by describing the different ways that these two kinds of responses were experimentally analyzed by (37)____________ and his students.

B. F. Skinner calls the kind of responses that *operate upon* a situation as well as respond to the situation (38)____________(*operants* or *respondents,* which would you guess?).

Operants operate upon a situation and sometimes seem to be uncaused—that is, they do not seem to be elicited by any specific (39)____________.

Operants sometimes do not seem to be elicited by any specific stimulus. Operants appear to be *emitted* (meaning "sent out") *by* the (40)____________ himself.

On the other hand, some responses are always *elicited* ("drawn out") *from* the individual by specific identifiable stimuli. Responses which are never *emitted* but always *elicited* are called (41)____________ (*operants* or *respondents*?).

Respondents are always elicited from the individual by specific identifiable stimuli. Respondents are *never* (42)____________.

Often, however, an individual *emits* responses. The kind of response that may be elicited but sometimes seems to be emitted by the individual is technically called (43)____________ (*operant* or *voluntary*?).

DIFFERENCES

Operants differ from respondents in many ways. There are some responses, however, that sometimes seem to be operant and sometimes to be respondent (*breathing* and *blinking* are examples of such responses). Some psychologists believe that every response is either operant or respondent and that there is a neurological or biochemical basis for the difference between operants and respondents.

Give an example of an operant: (44)____________

Give an example of a respondent: (45)________

As we have mentioned before, breathing and blinking are not good examples of either operant or respondent responses.

For each of the following statements tell whether it *best* seems to describe "operants" or "respondents":

Emitted *by the individual.* (46)________

Elicited *from the individual.* (47)________

Usually can *not* be controlled by spoken instructions or requests. (48)________

The form of the response often changes while the response-sequence is being learned. (49)________

There are unconditioned stimuli that will elicit the entire response without any previous learning. (50)________

The "same" response can be made in several different ways. (51)____________

Learning this type of response sometimes means learning a series of stimulus-response co-ordinations. (52)____________

Often what the response accomplishes is used as the name for the response. (53)____________

(All but 47, 48, and 50 are operant.)

The next three comparisons are a little more difficult:

Not a naturally automatic response to any stimulus but may *become* an automatic response to certain stimuli. (54)____________

When we say that an individual "learns" this kind of response, we *never* mean that he learns how to make a new kind of response, but that the same old kind of response is now elicited by different stimuli. (55)__________

Usually the specific change in some part of the individual is used as the name for the response. (56)__________

(54 is operant; 55 and 56 are respondent.)

SUMMARY

STUDY THE FOLLOWING DEFINITIONS CAREFULLY. LEARN THEM WELL. THEY ARE BASIC TO THE REST OF THE LESSONS IN THIS BOOK.

Respondent (a) A response for which there is at least one specific unconditioned stimulus.
(b) A response that consists of the same kind of change in the individual each time it happens.

Operant (a) A response for which there is no unconditioned stimulus.
(b) A response that is named and identified

according to the effect it has rather than according to how it is done (can usually be done in several different ways).

LESSON TEST: AFTER YOU HAVE COMPLETED THIS LESSON, ANSWER THE FOLLOWING QUESTIONS WITHOUT LOOKING BACK AT THE LESSON:

1. Who was the man who first defined the technical terms "operant" and "respondent"?
2. Name one operant that was discussed in this lesson.
3. Name one respondent that was discussed in this lesson.
4. The kind of response that usually *can not* be controlled by spoken instructions or requests is called ____________ (*operant* or *respondent*?).
5. The kind of response that is most likely to be called "voluntary" in everyday speech is technically called ____________ (*operant* or *respondent*?).
6. Respondents are always ____________ (*elicited* or *emitted*?).
7. Fear, hope, anger, love, and other emotions are all ____________ (*operants* or *respondents*?).
8. What are the two basic differences between operants and respondents according to the definitions at the end of this lesson? (If you do not know them already, memorize them now.)

CHECK YOUR ANSWERS (OR EXCHANGE ANSWERS AND CHECK) BY LOOKING BACK AT THE LESSON. CAREFULLY CORRECT EVERY MISTAKE OR OMISSION.

PART II

Respondent

LESSON 5

Respondents

[Estimated time: 35 minutes]

> Our experiments have been performed exclusively on the dog, in which the particular reaction was an unimportant physiologic process—the secretion of saliva. . . . Saliva flows, as we all know, when something is given the dog to eat or is introduced forcibly into his mouth.
>
> . . . . .
>
> Any visual stimulus, any desired sound, any odour, and the stimulation of any part of the skin, either by mechanical means or by the application of heat or cold, have never failed in our hands to stimulate the salivary glands, although before they were all ineffective for that purpose. This was accomplished by applying the stimuli simultaneously with the action of the salivary glands, their action having been evoked by giving of certain kinds of food, or by forcing certain substances into the dog's mouth.
>
> —I. P. PAVLOV[1]

An old English proverb about fire says: "The burned child fears the (1)______________."

[1] *Lectures on Conditioned Reflexes*, Vol. I, trans. W. H. Gantt (New York: International Publishers, 1928), pp. 83, 86.

The sight and sound of fire frighten the child who has been (2)__________ by fire.

A child is hurt by being burned. The child responds. Without any learning at all, a burn will elicit certain (3)__________ (*operants* or *respondents*?).

A burn on the hand *elicits respondents* such as heart beating faster, mouth becoming dry, and twitch of the fingers. However, a little baby whose hand is being burned *will not necessarily move its hand away.* Moving away is (4)__________ (*operant* or *respondent*?).

An operant is a response for which there (5)__________ (*is an unconditioned stimulus* or *is no unconditioned stimulus*?).

An operant is a response for which there is no unconditioned stimulus.

UNCONDITIONED STIMULI

An unconditioned stimulus-action is a stimulus-action that elicits a response that an individual (6)__________(*had to learn* or *did not learn*?) how to make.

An individual does not learn how to make a respondent response. Respondents are elicited without any conditioning by *unconditioned* (7)______________ (*proper stimuli* or *stimulus-actions*?).

"Unconditioned" means (8)______________ (*after* or *without*?) respondent conditioning.

An unconditioned stimulus-action for a respondent is a stimulus-action that elicits that response without (9)______________.

Conditioning is a type of learning. *Unconditioned* means "*without respondent conditioning.*" A stimulus-action that without learning will elicit a respondent is called (10)______________ (*a conditioned* or *an unconditioned*?) stimulus-action for that respondent.

DEFINITION: *An* unconditioned *stimulus-action for a respondent is a stimulus-action that will elicit that respondent without any conditioning being needed.*

Respondents such as heart beating faster and mouth drying up are elicited from an individual when he is burned. The burn is (11)______________ (*a conditioned* or *an unconditioned*?) stimulus for these respondents.

Every proper stimulus is an unconditioned stimulus for some (12)____________ (*operant* or *respondent*?).

Every proper stimulus is an unconditioned stimulus for some respondent. A stimulus-action, however, may elicit the respondent for which it is an unconditioned stimulus and *also elicit other respondents* for which it has become a conditioned stimulus, *and guide operants* for which it is a discriminative stimulus (i.e., the same stimulus-action may come to have many effects at once).

CONDITIONED STIMULI

If a child is badly burned, the child's mouth may dry up in the future whenever it sees a (13)____________.

Fire is a stimulus-agent. Changes in the fire and changes in the relationship between an individual and the fire are stimulus-events. If an individual responds in some way to these stimulus-events, they are stimulus-(14)____________ upon that individual.

A stimulus-action is an (15)____________ (*agent* or *event*?) that elicits or changes a response.

A stimulus-action is an event that elicits or changes a response. All stimuli are not stimulus-actions. Events and agents around an individual that are proper stimuli or experimenters' stimuli are stimuli; but they may not be stimulus-(16)________.

After respondent conditioning, sight and sound of fire become (17)________ (*conditioned* or *unconditioned*?) stimuli for respondents such as mouth drying up or heart beating faster.

A conditioned stimulus-action for a respondent is a stimulus-action that (18)________ (*would* or *would not*?) usually elicit that respondent from a newborn baby.

DEFINITION: A conditioned *stimulus-action for a respondent is a stimulus-action that would not normally elicit that respondent before respondent conditioning but does elicit it after conditioning.*

Conditioned means (19)________ (*after* or *without*?) respondent conditioning.

Conditioned means "after (20)________ conditioning."

RESPONDENT CONDITIONING

DEFINITION: Respondent conditioning *is the name for the process by which a stimulus-action becomes conditioned to elicit a respondent by being associated with that respondent.*

In some discussions of respondent conditioning it is said that the stimulus to be conditioned is conditioned by being associated with the unconditioned stimulus. This is *partially* true. That is, it is true if by "stimulus" we always mean (21)______________ (*experimenters' stimulus, proper stimulus*, or *stimulus-action*?).

An uncondtioned stimulus-action for one respondent also becomes a conditioned stimulus-action *for another respondent* by occurring at the same time as (that is, by accompanying) the other (22)______________ (*respondent* or *stimulus*?), thereby being associated with it.

The important association in respondent conditioning is the association *between the two respondents* (*not* between two stimuli), so that a stimulus-action that previously elicited only one of the respondents now elicits both (23)______________.

Stimulus-actions that occur at the same time as a respondent (a respondent that *they did not elicit*) are *associated* with that respondent *and become* (24) ____________ (*conditioned* or *unconditioned*?) stimuli for that respondent.

A stimulus-action becomes conditioned to a respondent by being (25)____________ with that respondent.

After the sight of fire has been associated with the pain of being burned, an individual will fear the sight of fire. We call this (26)____________ conditioning.

Respondent conditioning (27)____________ (*does* or *does not*?) mean a change in the form of the respondent (that is, a change in the *way* the response is made).

Respondent conditioning does *not* mean a change in the respondent. Respondents are defined as responses that usually (28)____________ (*do* or *do not*?) change in form.

When we say that someone "learns" a respondent we *never* mean that he learns *how* to make a new kind of response.

There is always some stimulus-action that (29)____________ (*elicits* or *produces*?) a respondent.

Respondents are elicited without conditioning by (30)__________ (*conditioned* or *unconditioned*?) stimuli.

During respondent conditioning a stimulus that is an unconditioned stimulus for one respondent also becomes a conditioned stimulus for another respondent. Therefore, respondent conditioning (31)__________ (*decreases* or *increases*?) the number of respondents elicited by the stimlus that is conditioned.

Respondent conditioning usually increase the number of respondents elicited by the stimulus that is conditioned because the conditioned stimulus continues to be an unconditioned stimulus for its unconditioned response.

RESPONDENTS AND OPERANTS ARE QUITE DIFFERENT

Unconditioned stimuli elicit (32)__________ (*operants* or *respondents*?).

Unconditioned stimuli elicit respondents. Conditioned stimuli also elicit respondents. Conditioned stimuli *never* elicit (33)__________.

Operants are *never* elicited by conditioned stimuli. Operants are *never* elicited by unconditioned stimuli. Operants are *emitted* by the individual, *not elicited* from him. When a stimulus affects operants, it is called a "discriminative stimulus." We shall study discriminative stimuli when we study operant conditioning.

Respondent conditioning is the name for the process by which a stimulus becomes conditioned to elicit a respondent for which it is not an (34)__________ stimulus.

Unconditioned stimuli and conditioned stimuli both elicit respondents. An unconditioned stimulus for one respondent also becomes a conditioned stimulus for another respondent by being associated with the other (35)__________.

In respondent conditioning a stimulus-action becomes conditioned to elicit a respondent by being (36)__________ with this respondent.

When a stimulus-action is associated with a respondent that it did not elicit, the stimulus-action becomes conditioned to this respondent and in the future this stimulus-action will tend to (37)__________ (*elicit, emit,* or *produce*?) this respondent.

A stimulus-action elicits both its unconditioned response and any other respondent to which it has been conditioned.

SOME ABBREVIATIONS

Instead of writing out "a conditioned stimulus" we often use the abbreviation (38)______________ (*CS* or *UCS*, which would you choose?).

CS stands for "a conditioned stimulus" and UCS stands for "an (39)______________ stimulus."

Another common abbreviation is S. S stands for (40)______________(*experimenter* or *subject*?).

E stands for "experimenter."

REVIEW

No respondent ever occurs all alone. S is always responding in many ways at the same time. The total response of an individual can always be analyzed into many different individual respondents. Sometimes we have a name for a set of respondents that occur together under certain circumstances. Excitement, fear, joy, pain, and other emotional responses involve patterns made up of many respondents (changes in heart rate, salivation, skin resistance, pupillary size, glandular secretion, digestive processes, and so forth).

Different names may be assigned to the same set of respondents, depending on what the eliciting stimuli are.

The pattern of respondents elicited by a severe burn is called pain; the same pattern of responses elicited by the sight of a fire is called fear.

A severe burn is (41)____________ (*CS* or *UCS*?) for pain.

Sight of fire may become (42)____________ (*CS* or *UCS*?) for fear.

Severe burn is UCS and sight of fire may become CS for these responses. We call the total response (43)____________ (*fear* or *pain*?) when a severe burn elicits it. The same total response can be elicited by a CS. If a CS elicits the response, however, we call the response (44)____________ (*fear* or *pain*?).

LESSON TEST: AFTER YOU HAVE COMPLETED THIS LESSON ANSWER THE FOLLOWING QUESTIONS WITHOUT LOOKING BACK AT THE LESSON:

1. The two basic differences that distinguish operants from respondents are whether or not there is a UCS for the response and whether or not the response can change in form.
   Operants____________.

2. "Respondent conditioning" is the name for the process by which a stimulus-action becomes conditioned to elicit a respondent by ____________.

3. Define "unconditional stimulus" and "conditioned stimulus."

4. Tears coming into a person's eyes is a respondent. The smell of freshly cut raw onions will usually elicit this respondent. How might someone condition this respondent so that the sound of a bell would elicit it? In this conditioning, the smell of the onions is the ___________ and the sound of the bell is the ___________.

CHECK YOUR ANSWERS (OR EXCHANGE ANSWERS AND CHECK) BY LOOKING BACK AT THE LESSON. CAREFULLY CORRECT EVERY MISTAKE OR OMISSION.

PROJECT II

Experimental Analysis of a Respondent

> If you want a specified behavior from yourself, set up the conditions which you know will control it.
>
> —I. GOLDIAMOND[1]

Pavlov, an internationally famous Russian *physiologist*, was the first man to study respondent conditioning. His experiments with respondent conditioning have been repeated and studied by psychologists even more than they have by physiologists.

Pavlov showed that any stimulus-action which occurs at about the same time as a respondent will become CS for that respondent. In the quotation at the beginning of Lesson 5 he describes his general procedure. CS (usually either a visual stimulus or a sound) is presented to S while, at the same time, increased salivation is elicited by UCS (usually food or mild acid). After CS has accompanied salivation, it begins to elicit salivation itself even when presented without UCS.

Most of us find that our mouths "dry up" when fire is brought close to our faces. If we were suddenly to try "fire

[1] "Self-control procedures in personal behavior problems," *Psychol. Rev.* (1965), *17*:853.

eating" after watching a carnival demonstration, we would quite likely be badly burned. The professional "fire-eater" is not burned because he maintains normal salivation while the fire is in his mouth, and his saliva protects the inner surfaces of his mouth from the flame.

Pavlov did all of his conditioning with dogs as Ss. It is not possible for this book to provide a dog for you. It is possible, however, for a human being to learn to control one of his own respondents. Thus, in a sense, he gains operant control over a respondent. For example, if I want my mouth not to dry up when a flame comes close, I must find some way to make myself salivate normally so that the sight and feel of the fire will become CS for normal salivation instead of CS for mouth drying up. One way to do this is to look at a small flame far away and then slowly to move the flame closer. If I stop for a short time whenever the flame starts to make my mouth dry up, I will become accustomed to the fire being nearer and nearer while I still have normal salivation.

Several hundred students were assigned the following project while this book was being written. A very few of these students found that they were not ready to go beyond step 3 (and did not go beyond step 3) as their mouths continued to dry up at the sight of a match burning near their faces. Most students completed step 6 successfully; less than half did step 8. No student ever reported any more than slight discomfort as a result of this project.

Carefully read over *all* of this lesson *before starting* the project.

PURPOSE: To explore the possibility of a person controlling his own salivation so that normal salivation continues when he puts a burning match or small torch into his mouth. (Some psychologists, such as the author of this book, would call this respondent conditioning—or, at least, counterconditioning. Many psychologists would call this a demonstration of respondent extinction. We shall briefly define and discuss extinction in Lesson 11.)

MATERIALS: A box or package of matches.

PROCEDURE:

1. Light a match and examine it while holding it in front of you. It may be necessary for you to do this several times before you can do it without being aware of any change in your normal salivation (the normal wetness of the inside of your mouth).

2. When you are certain that you can light a match and hold it in front of you without making your mouth dry up at all, bring the match up to a few inches from your mouth. Look at the match carefully. (It might help you if you think of good things to eat that must be cooked.) *Remember,* there is no normal salivation on the outside of your mouth and you can be burned there at any time. *Be careful not to advance to closer contact with the flame until you are certain that the earlier steps did not make your mouth dry up.*

3. Move an *unlighted* match in and out of your mouth.

4. When you are certain that you can hold a lighted match for a few seconds a few inches from your open mouth without making your mouth dry up and you can put an unlighted match in and out of your mouth without making your mouth dry up, *then* move a lighted match quickly and briefly in and out of your open mouth.

5. After you have moved a lighted match quickly and

briefly in and out of your mouth several times, you will be able to do it without it making your mouth dry up. (You may need to try this several different times, perhaps even on different days.) *Then* insert a lighted match into your mouth and leave it in slightly longer each time until you can hold the match in your mouth for *one* or *two* seconds. (Our intention is *not* to attempt to manage any long intervals.)

6. When you are certain that you can hold a lighted match in your mouth for one or two seconds without it making your mouth dry up, put a match into your mouth and briefly close your lips slightly over it.

7. After the first six steps have been completed you may be able to use several matches at a time or a small paper torch. Take care not to make any large change at any one time and remember that (1) the outside of your mouth has no protection; and (2) "normal" salivation is still not a large amount of saliva, and the more fire the more quickly the flame will dry up your saliva.

8. *After* you have successfully completed all of the steps above without any burn, you *might* try a final step. If you are able to maintain normal saliva when a flame is in your mouth for a brief periods of time, you can also put a match out against your tongue!

COMMENT: In this project we do not want to increase salivation but to maintain normal salivation under unusual conditions. Therefore we do not need any UCS. Many minor fears can be removed by following this same procedure. The *danger* of the procedure when used to remove fears *is* the same as the danger in this project: the danger that you will burn yourself as a result of *proceeding too fast.*

REPORT:

Part I. Write what happened when you tried this project.

Part II. In this project you tried to learn not to be afraid when you put a flame into your mouth. To do this you used a respondent conditioning procedure on yourself. Think of some other fear that you have or that someone you know has. Tell what the fear is and how it might be removed by respondent conditioning.

LESSON 6

Conditioned Stimuli

[Estimated time: 20 minutes]

Writing in 1890, William James stoutly supported the then current supposition that anxiety was an *instinctive* ("idiopathic") reaction to certain objects or situations, which might or might not represent real danger. . . .

Some years later John B. Watson (1928) demonstrated experimentally that, contrary to the Jamesian view, most human fears are specifically relatable to and dependent upon individual experience. Starting with the reaction of infants to loud sounds or loss of physical support . . . Watson was able to show, by means of Pavlov's conditioning technique, that an indefinitely wide range of other stimuli, if associated with this reaction, could be made to acquire the capacity to elicit unmistakably fearful behavior. . . . According to Watson's observations, human infants show no innate *fear* responses whatever, merely innate *pain* responses.

Freud seems to have seen the problem in this light from the outset and accordingly posited that *all* anxiety (fear) reactions are probably learned. . . . In short, *anxiety (fear) is the conditioned form of the pain reaction,* which has the highly useful function of motivating and reinforcing behavior that tends to avoid or prevent the recurrence of the pain-producing (unconditioned) stimulus.

—O. H. MOWRER[1]

1 "A stimulus-response analysis of anxiety and its role as a reinforcing agent," *Psychol. Rev.* (1939), *46*:563–565.

The above quotation tells a portion of the history of an important problem. O. H. Mowrer reviews the positions of William James, John B. Watson, and then the position of the famous founder of psychoanalysis, Sigmund (1)____________.

Freud's clinical experience and Watson's experiments seem to lead to the conclusion stated by Mowrer that *"anxiety (fear) is the conditioned form of the* (2)____________ *reaction."*

The observation that stimuli that have accompanied pain will later themselves tend to elicit fear is really not new. "Once bitten, twice shy" is an old English folk saying. We learn to fear things that have hurt us in the past. Responses such as digestive processes stopping, mouth drying up, heart beating faster, and eye pupils contracting, are the responses of fear and pain. These responses are (3)____________ (*operant* or *respondent*?).

"Once bitten, twice shy" also has another meaning. We usually try to keep from being hurt. When something has hurt us in the past, we tend to try to avoid it. Responses such as running away, hiding, or standing still so that we will not be noticed may help us to avoid being bitten (or hurt in some other way). These responses are (4)____________ (*operant* or *respondent*?).

We must learn both *how* to make the right operant and *when* to make it. We do *not learn how* to make respondents. Respondents, however, are often (5)________ to stimuli that would not unconditionally elicit them.

Respondent conditioning is the name for the process by which a stimulus-action becomes conditioned to elicit a respondent by being (6)__________ *with that respondent.*

The child who has been bitten by a dog fears dogs because the child associates dogs with the pain of being bitten.

FEAR AS AN ACQUIRABLE DRIVE

In 1948 Neal E. Miller reported the following experiment:

> Albino rats were placed in a simple apparatus consisting of two compartments separated by a door. One was white with a grid as a floor; the other was black without a grid. Before training, the animals showed no marked preference for either compartment. Then they were placed in the white compartment, received an electric shock from the grid, and escaped into the black compartment through the open door. After a number of such trials, the animals would run out of the white compartment even if no shock was on the grid.
>
> To demonstrate that an acquired drive (fear or anxiety) had been established, the animals were taught a *new* habit *without further shocks*. The door (previously always open) was closed. The only way that the door could be opened was by rotating a little wheel, which was above

the door, a fraction of a turn. Under these conditions, the animals exhibited trial-and-error behavior and gradually learned to escape from the white compartment by rotating the wheel.

If conditions were changed so that only pressing a bar would open the door, wheel turning extinguished, and a second new habit (bar pressing) was learned.

—N. E. MILLER[2]

In this famous study by Neal E. Miller, the experienced rats became emotionally upset as soon as they were put into the white compartment. Becoming emotionally upset is (7) ______________ (*operant* or *respondent*?).

Becoming emotionally upset is respondent and learning to become emotionally upset (to become afraid) whenever a subject is put into a certain place is an example of (8)______________ (*operant conditioning* or *respondent conditioning*?).

In this respondent conditioning, the UCS was (9)________. The CS was (10)______________.

The UCS was the electric shock, and the CS was the sight and smell, etc., of the white compartment.

2 "Studies of fear as an acquirable drive. I. Fear as motivation and fear-reduction as reinforcement in the learning of new responses," *J. exp. Psychol.* (1948), 38:89–101.

The rats learned to run out of the white compartment as soon as they were put in. Running is (11)________ (*an operant* or *a respondent*?).

When a rat *no longer ever received any electric shock,* it still continued to run from the white compartment into the black compartment whenever it was put into the white compartment. Although they received no more shocks, 13 of the 25 experimental animals learned to move the wheel when they had to move the wheel in order to open the door out of the white compartment. Turning a wheel is (12)____________ (*operant* or *respondent*?).

Of the 13 rats who learned to turn the wheel, 12 learned to press a bar, instead, when the experiment was changed so that turning the wheel would no longer open the door; but the door opened whenever the bar was pressed. These rats learned to press the bar to get out of the white compartment because they (13)__________ (*were being hurt in the white compartment* or *were afraid of the white compartment*?).

The rats were never shocked after the preliminary respondent conditioning. They did not learn to turn the wheel and later press the bar to get out of the white compartment because they were still being hurt in the white compartment. They learned to do these things because they were now afraid of the white compartment. As Miller puts it ". . . this experiment confirms Mowrer's hypothesis that fear (or anxiety) can play a role in learning similar to that of a primary drive such as hunger." (*Op. cit.*, p. 98.)

VALUES

Our specific fears, hopes, goals, and values are (14)______________ (*inherited* or *learned*?).

An infant is born with certain very definite needs, but both the what and the how of fulfilling these needs to a great extent must be learned. Learning what things bring pain and what things bring relief is primarily a matter of (15)______________ conditioning.

Respondent conditioning is the name for the process by which a stimulus-action becomes conditioned to elicit a respondent by being associated with that respondent. Feelings and emotions are respondent, not operant. Our specific fears, hopes, goals, and values are at least to a great extent the result of respondent conditioning.

If human beings are to live in communities and raise children, their value systems must develop far beyond the means for protecting themselves as individuals and fulfilling individual needs:

> . . . besides the happiness and the security of the individuals of whom the community is at any moment composed, there are also the happiness and the security of the individuals of whom generation after generation it will be composed. . . . That is why young men die in battle for

their country's sake and why old men plant trees they will never sit under.

—WALTER LIPPMANN[3]

Being willing to die for the things in which you believe and planting trees that you will never sit under both require that a person have a background that involves more than simple respondent conditioning. Perhaps that is the reason for such behaviors not being more common than they are.

UNCONDITIONED STIMULI

Some responses have unconditioned stimuli, some do not. Which of the following responses have unconditioned stimuli? (16)__________

1. Walking
2. Salivation (increasing the amount of water coming from glands in the mouth)
3. Talking
4. Contraction of eye pupil (dark portion in middle of the eye surface becoming smaller)
5. Putting on the brake in an automobile

Each of these responses under particular circumstances might be a response to the ringing of a bell. For which of these responses would the sound of the bell be a *conditioned* stimulus and for which would it be a *discriminative* stimulus?

[3] *The Public Philosophy* (Boston: Little Brown, 1955), pp. 35 ff.

Walking (17)__________

Salivation (18)__________

Talking (19)__________

Contraction of eye pupil (20)__________

Putting on the brake in an automobile (21)__________

A conditioned stimulus is a stimulus that elicits a respondent after respondent conditioning. No operant can have a conditioned stimulus. Operants are responses to discriminative stimuli (that indicate what events are likely to follow what operants). Salivation and contraction of eye pupil have unconditioned stimuli and can have conditioned stimuli. Walking, talking, and putting on the brake in an automobile are operants and do not have unconditioned stimuli or conditioned stimuli. They are responses to discriminative stimuli.

RESPONDENTS AND OPERANTS

No operant has a UCS. No operant has a CS. An operant, however, may be learned so well that it is automatically elicited by the occurrence of the familiar situation. Does this make it a respondent? (22)__________

The fact that an operant has become automatic does *not* make it respondent. Many complex operants are necessary in order to play a good game of tennis or to land an airplane. These operants may be quite automatic once you have learned, *but they are still* (23)____________

Operants may become automatic, but they are still operant. A simpler example is jerking your hand away from a hot stove or from some painful source of stimulation. Jerking your hand away at such times is quite automatic for most of us. If a baby's hand is burned, however, it may not move its hand at all, or it may press its hand even harder against the source of the pain! Jerking your hand away is (24)____________ (*operant* or *respondent*?).

Jerking your hand away is operant. We shall study a description of what happens as a baby learns this operant when we do the lesson on operant shaping.

Sometimes S's response to CS after respondent conditioning is somewhat different in form from S's response as it was to UCS before conditioning.

When this occurs, a possible explanation is that the response being recorded or observed is not a simple distinct respondent, but, at least in part, an (25)____________.

If a response is operant, we call the stimuli that produce it "discriminative stimuli." If a response is respondent, we call the stimuli that elicit it either (26)____________ stimuli or (27)____________ stimuli.

REVIEW

If a stimulus-action is to become CS for a respondent, it must accompany that (28)____________. ("Stimulus" is *not* the correct answer here!)

Respondent conditioning is the association of a stimulus-action to a respondent, *not* just the association of two (29)____________.

The fact that the stimulus that is supposed to become CS occurs at about the same time as UCS does not necessarily mean it will become CS.

For example, if an experimenter turns on a UCS, but somehow the UCS is not a (30)____________ upon the subject, there will certainly be no conditioning!

A stimulus-action must be associated with (i.e., happen at about the same time or slightly before) a respondent in order to become a (31)____________ for that respondent.

"A cat that happens to jump onto a hot stove lid is not likely ever to do so again. In fact this cat may become emotionally upset in the future whenever it sees a stove lid."

Jumping is the kind of response we call (12)__________ (*operant* or *respondent*?). Emotional upset, on the other hand, is the kind of response we call (33)______________ (*operant* or *respondent*?).

Having your feet badly burned is (34)______________ (*CS* or *UCS*?) for emotional upset.

Having your feet badly burned is an unconditioned stimulus for emotional upset. For the cat in the quotation, sight of any stove lid has probably become a (35)______________ stimulus for emotional upset as a result of (36)______________ (*operant* or *respondent*?) conditioning.

LESSON TEST: AFTER YOU HAVE COMPLETED THIS LESSON, ANSWER THE FOLLOWING QUESTIONS WITHOUT LOOKING BACK AT THE LESSONS:

1. What are the two basic differences between operants and respondents?
2. Define "respondent conditioning."
3. In English we sometimes have two words that mean exactly the same thing, except that one of the words,

(a), is likely to be used in textbooks and technical writing (and may occasionally be used in polite society), while the other word, (b), although it has exactly the same meaning, is *not* likely to be found in textbooks and is usually a forbidden word in polite society. One example is the pair (a) excreta, (b) shit. Most students will be familiar with other such pairs. Hearing one of the "impolite" (b) words may make some people blush or elicit other respondents from them. These words are conditioned stimuli for such respondents (definitely not unconditioned stimuli). Give an example of such a word and of how it might have become CS for blushing or embarrassment.

CHECK YOUR ANSWER 2 BY LOOKING BACK AT LESSON 5.

CHECK YOUR ANSWER 3 BY DISCUSSING IT WITH SOMEONE ELSE WHO IS STUDYING THESE LESSONS.

PART III

Operant

LESSON 7

Operants

[Estimated time: 30 minutes]

> The word "operant" . . . emphasizes the fact that the behavior *operates* upon the environment to generate consequences. . . . In operant conditioning we "strengthen" an operant in the sense of making a response more probable or, in actual fact, more frequent.
>
> —B. F. SKINNER[1]

> The term voluntary is a misleading description of operant behavior because operants * * * [are] controlled through variables as completely as respondents.
>
> —JAMES G. HOLLAND AND B. F. SKINNER[2]

In 1937 B. F. Skinner presented a system for the description and analysis of the behavior of organisms based upon his distinction between two kinds of behavior: (1)____________ and (2)____________.

Operant behavior has been analyzed more extensively than respondent behavior in the laboratories of B. F. (3)____________ and his students.

1 *Science and Human Behavior* (New York: Macmillan, 1953), p. 65.
2 *The Analysis of Behavior* (New York: McGraw-Hill, 1961), p. 302.

Skinner's work has greatly advanced the science of psychology. It has had many applications in areas from education to psychopharmacology. Skinner takes the complex type of response that operates upon the environment, the (4)____________ (*operant* or *respondent*?) as his basic unit of analysis.

An operant is *produced* by the total situation. We say that the situation causes the individual to (5)________ (*elicit* or *emit*?) the operant.

We say that the general situation causes the individual to emit an operant, that the general situation (6)____________ (*emits* or *produces*?) the operant.

For example, a child may be taught that if he says "Please pass the potatoes" at the dinner table, someone will pass the potatoes to him. If he just says "Pass the potatoes," Mother or Dad will ask him to say "Please" and will not pass the potatoes until (7)____________.

Saying "Please" is an example of (8)____________ (*an operant* or *a respondent*?).

The individual (9)____________ (*elicits* or *emits*) operants.

The kind of responses that are not emitted by the individual, but are elicited from him by specific CSs or UCSs are called (10)__________.

Respondents are always elicited from the individual by specific CS or UCS. We have defined operants as responses for which there is no (11)__________ stimulus.

An operant is a response for which there is no unconditioned stimulus (and, therefore, no conditioned stimulus either!). Operants (12)__________ (*never* or *often*?) change in form.

An operant is a response that can be done in several different ways and usually (13)__________ (*can* or *can not*?) be controlled by spoken instructions or requests.

The kind of response for which there is an unconditioned stimulus is a response that does not change in form and usually can not be controlled by spoken instructions or requests. This kind of response is called (14)__________.

REINFORCING CONSEQUENCES

How often an individual will emit an operant in a situation depends mainly on what *consequences have followed such operants* in the past in similar situations. A *reinforcing consequence* of an operant is an event that happens after the individual emits the operant and (15)______________ (*decreases* or *increases*?) the probability that the individual will make this type of operant again in future similar situations.

A consequence of an operant that increases the probability that the individual will emit that type of operant again in future similar situations is called a (16)____________ (*reinforcing* or *rewarding*?) consequence.

"Reinforcing consequences" are not the same thing as "rewards." Sometimes events or agents are designated as "rewards" because the person giving them considers them to be desirable; sometimes events or agents are called "rewards" because the person receiving them considers them to be desirable. The individual doing the giving and the individual doing the receiving do not always agree as to what is desirable (or even always agree what "desirable" means).

Events are "reinforcing" *only if they follow an operant and* (17)______________ the probability that the individual will repeat this type of operant in future similar situations.

DEFINITION: *A* reinforcing consequence *of an operant is an event that happens after the operant and increases the probabilty that this type of operant will be repeated in future similar situations.*

Reinforcing consequences (18)____________ (*are* or *are not*?) the same thing as rewards.

REINFORCERS

More than one kind of event can be reinforcing. The *onset* (that is, the start, presentation, or appearance) of some things is likely to be reinforcing. When you are cold, for example, the *onset* of heat is likely to be a (19)____________ consequence for any operant you make that is followed by heat.

The *termination* (that is, the stopping, removal, or disappearance) of some other things is more likely to be reinforcing than their onset. When your foot is in a painfully tight shoe, *termination* of the pressure is likely to be a (20)____________ for any operant you make that is followed by relief from pain.

A *positive* reinforcer is an *agent* whose (21)__________ (*onset* or *termination,* which would you guess?) is a reinforcing consequence for operants that it follows.

DEFINITION: *A positive reinforcer* is an *agent* whose *onset* is a *reinforcing consequence for operants that it follows.*

A negative reinforcer is an *agent* whose (22)________ (*onset* or *termination*?) is a reinforcing consequence for operants that it follows.

DEFINITION: *A negative reinforcer* is an *agent* whose *termination* after an *operant* is a *reinforcing consequence for that operant.*

Electric shock, for instance, is an agent whose termination is usually reinforcing for operants. Electric shock is thus usually a (23)______________ reinforcer.

Electric shock usually is a negative reinforcer. In a situation in which S gets a painful shock through the feet every few minutes, if S finds that the shock stops whenever he presses a bar in the wall, frequency of bar pressing will usually (24)____________ (*decrease* or *increase*?).

Frequency of bar pressing will increase in situations in which each bar press is followed by a (25)________ (*reinforcing* or *rewarding*?) consequence.

A reinforcing consequence is defined as an event that happens after an operant and increases the (26)__________ that this type of operant will be repeated in future similar situations.

The probabilty that the operant will be emitted in future similar situations is (27)____________ when the operant is followed by a reinforcing consequence.

To put it another way, the frequency with which an operant will be repeated will increase in situations in which a reinforcing consequence occurs each time the individual emits the operant.

(28)____________ (*onset* or *termination*?) of the sight of food is likely to be a reinforcing consequence.

Onset of the sight of food is a reinforcing consequence if the individual is at all hungry. Food, in this case, is a (29)____________ reinforcer.

When an operant is followed by a reinforcing consequence each time it occurs, the frequency of this operant will (30)____________.

OPERANT CONDITIONING

Increase in frequency with which an individual makes the operant in situations in which such operants are followed by reinforcing consequences is called (31)________ conditioning.

Operant conditioning is the name for the process by which a behavioral situation comes to produce a certain type of operant (32)______________ (*more and more often* or *less and less often*?).

DEFINITION: Operant conditioning *is the name for the process by which a behavioral situation comes to produce a certain type of operant by the individual more and more frequently when such operants are followed by reinforcing consequences.*

Respondent conditioning is the name for the process by which a stimulus becomes conditioned to elicit a respondent by being associated with that (33)__________.

Respondent conditioning is the name for the process by which a stimulus becomes conditioned to elicit a respondent by being (34)____________ with that respondent.

Operant conditioning is the name for the process by which a (35)____________ (*behavioral* or *physical*?) situation comes to produce a certain type of operant by the individual more and more frequently.

Operant conditioning is the name for the process by which a behavioral situation comes to produce a certain type of operant by the individual more and more frequently in situations in which such operants are followed by (36)____________ consequences.

A SUMMARY TO MEMORIZE

Operant conditioning occurs in a situation in which some operants are followed by reinforcing consequences and other operants are not followed by reinforcing consequences. The operants that are followed by reinforcing consequences are emitted more often in that situation.

Respondent conditioning occurs when a stimulus-action becomes a conditioned stimulus for a respondent by being associated with the respondent.

DISCRIMINATIVE STIMULI

An event may be UCS for one respondent and CS for (37)____________ (*an operant, another respondent*?).

Respondents are elicited from the individual by UCSs and CSs. *There is no such thing as a UCS or a CS for an* (38)____________.

Operants are not elicited by UCSs or CSs. Operants are usually emitted by the individual. An individual, however, is likely to emit a certain kind of operant more often in situations in which such operants are followed by reinforcing (39)____________.

DEFINITION: A discriminative *stimulus (abbreviated* S^D*) is a stimulus that indicates to the individual what operants will bring about what events in this situation.*

Discriminative stimuli tell the individual what to do (what operants to emit). Spoken or printed words, signs, smells, sounds, sights, and so forth—all stimuli that guide and control operants by an individual—are (40)____________ stimuli for that individual.

Discriminative stimuli tell an individual what he must do to get what he wants. The abbreviation for "discriminative stimulus" is (41)____________.

Being S^D for an operant is quite different from being CS for a (42)____________.

A CS for a respondent is a stimulus-action that has been conditioned to elicit that respondent. An S^D indicates what events are likely to follow what (43)__________.

The way an S^D affects its kind of response (operants) is different from the way a UCS or CS affects its kind (respondents). The same stimulus, however, (44)__________ (*can* or *can not*, which would you guess?) be CS and S^D at the same time

The smell of a roast cooking, for example, can both elicit salivation and indicate that it is about time to go into the dining room for dinner.

LESSON TEST: AFTER YOU HAVE COMPLETED THIS LESSON, ANSWER THE FOLLOWING QUESTIONS WITHOUT LOOKING BACK AT THE LESSON:

1. *Operant conditioning* is the name for the process by which a behavioral situation comes to produce a certain type of operant by the individual more and more frequently when __________.
2. What is a negative reinforcer? If you had a splinter in your finger and got it out by soaking the finger in warm water, what was the negative reinforcer?
3. The most obvious difference between S^Ds and CSs is that S^Ds affect __________ (*operants* or *respondents?*), whereas CSs affect __________ (*operants* or *respondents?*).

4. What is the difference between a discriminative stimulus and a reinforcing consequence?

5. Give an example from your own experience in which you responded to a discriminative stimulus and received a reinforcing consequence.

CHECK YOUR ANSWERS (OR EXCHANGE ANSWERS AND CHECK) BY LOOKING BACK AT LESSON. CAREFULLY CORRECT EVERY MISTAKE OR OMISSION.

PROJECT III

Experimental Analysis of an Operant

> We are always reinforcing the behavior of others, whether we mean to be or not. A familiar problem is that of the child who seems to take an almost pathological delight in annoying its parents. In many cases this is the result of conditioning.
>
> . . . . .
>
> The mother may unwillingly promote the very behavior she does not want. For example, when she is busy she is likely not to respond to a call or request made in a quiet tone of voice. The average intensity of the child's vocal behavior therefore moves up to another level. . . . Eventually the mother gets used to this level and again reinforces only louder instances. This vicious circle brings about louder and louder behavior. . . . The mother behaves, in fact, as if she has been given the assignment of teaching the child to be annoying!
>
> —B. F. SKINNER[1]

Drawing a line on a piece of paper is a response for which there is no UCS, and it is possible to draw a line in many different ways (for example: holding the pencil

1 "How to Teach Animals," *Scientific American* (1951) *185*:26–29.

in your right hand, in your left hand, with your right foot, with your left foot, or in your mouth; drawing the line toward yourself, away from yourself, sidewise). Drawing a line is definitely an operant. Line drawing is the operant we shall use for analysis in this lesson.

If I have no ruler or other way to measure, I can not know exactly how long any line is. If someone asks me to draw a line 138 millimeters long, I will have to guess how long 138 mm is. Except for the effects of such things as getting tired, I will tend to draw a second line of about the same length as my first line if I am asked to draw another line 138 mm long. Even hundreds of repetitions will not change my behavioral situation so that I will begin to draw lines exactly 138 mm long. An old English proverb says "Practice makes perfect." The proverb is not true!

Being told "good" usually is a reinforcing consequence. It can also be a discriminative stimulus. If I am told that something I have done is good, I am likely to try to do it again. If I am trying to learn to draw a line 138 mm long and my teacher says "good" after I draw a line, I am likely to draw the next line about the same length. If my teacher says "good" whenever I draw a line that is a little bit shorter than the last line I drew, I am likely to draw a shorter line next time. When someone says "good" to me, this changes my behavioral situation. By saying "good" at the right times my teacher can help me to learn to draw lines 138 mm long.

PURPOSE: To observe how an operant (drawing a line) can be guided by the verbal stimulus (spoken word) "good."

MATERIALS: Pencil, straightedge guide of some sort (a book, a piece of cardboard, a ruler, or some other means

"Boy, have I got this guy conditioned! Every time I press the bar down he drops in a piece of food." (Adapted from a drawing that originally appeared in the *Columbia Jester.*)

IN DEMONSTRATIONS OF OPERANT CONDITIONING OF A SUBJECT BY A PSYCHOLOGIST, IT IS NOT ALWAYS CLEAR WHETHER THE PSYCHOLOGIST IS CONTROLLING THE ANIMAL OR WHETHER THE ANIMAL IS CONTROLLING THE PSYCHOLOGIST.

of providing a guide in drawing a straight line), a sheet of lined paper, and a table or other flat surface.

PROCEDURE: Ask someone to help you with this project. *In Part A you will be S* and your *friend* will be *E*. Then in *Part B, you* will be *E* and your *friend* will be *S*. These instructions should be read by both *E* and *S*.

Part A: The lined paper is put in front of *S*. *S* takes the pencil in his hand and puts the point of the pencil on the bottom line near the left edge of the paper. *E* tells *S* to draw *one* line, using the straightedge so that the line is straight. *E* must decide how long (how many of the printed lines on the lined paper) a "correct" line is to be. Then *E* will tell *S* to draw another line beside his first line. *S*'s problem is to find out how long a line *E* has decided is "correct."

After *S* has drawn his second line, *S* and *E* must not talk to each other. *E* will say "good" whenever *S* draws a "*correct*" line *and whenever S draws a line that is closer* to the "correct" length *than the last line S drew. E* will not say anything when *S* draws a line that is farther away from the "correct" line than the last line *S* drew. *S* must not talk at all. *S* will continue to draw lines until he has drawn three "correct" lines.

Part B: Now *E* and *S* change places and repeat *Part A* with the new *E* and the new *S* and a new "correct" length.

When the new *S* has drawn the "correct" length of line three times, *E* might see if he can shape more complicated operants. Without doing anything but say "good," some student *E*'s will be able to get *S* to draw mountains and valleys or other patterns of lines.

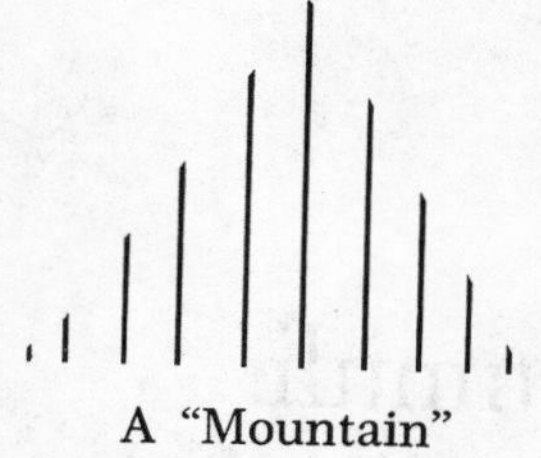

A "Mountain"

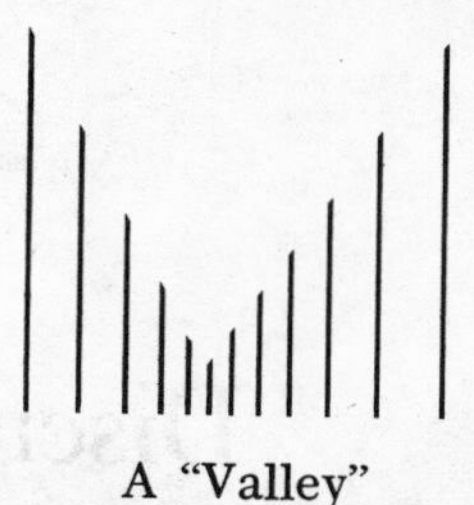

A "Valley"

COMMENT: In most human teaching and leadership situations we use many more stimuli than we were allowed to use in this project. We give *S* many other S^Ds and different reinforcers than just the word "good." However, in animal training and in some human training situations, a teacher or *E* may have to act about like the *E*'s in this project. (In animal studies instead of saying "good" we usually give *S* a bit of food or a little water as the reinforcing consequence of a "better" or a "correct" response.)

Operants are made by an individual in response to the situation in which he finds himself. If *E* is to bring about a situation such that *S* will make the operants *E* wants, *E* must give *S* positive reinforcers as effects of this kind of operant. This means that *E* must be controlled by what *S* does! (Look again at the drawing from the *Columbia Jester*.)

REPORT:

Part I. Write out what happened when you tried this project. In your report include the papers on which the lines were drawn. Carefully label the papers to show who is *E* and who is *S*.

Part II. Give a clear and specific example of how you might use operant conditioning techniques to teach someone some more useful skill than drawing "correct" lines.

LESSON

8

Discriminative Stimuli

[Estimated time: 25 minutes]

The control by the environment over the child's behavior depends first upon the emission of the behavior. This follows from the manner in which the environment comes to control the child's performance: the successful execution of an act on one occasion, coupled with the unsuccessful act in its absence.

—CHARLES B. FERSTER[1]

A (1)__________ (*conditioned stimulus, discriminative stimulus,* or *reinforcing consequence*?) tells you what to do and a (2)__________ (*conditioned stimulus, discriminative stimulus,* or *reinforcing consequence*?) is supposed to happen if you do it correctly.

A discriminative stimulus tells you what to do and a reinforcing consequence sometimes happens if you do it correctly. A discriminative stimulus indicates what events are likely to follow what (3)__________ (*operants* or *respondents*?).

1 "Positive reinforcement and behavioral deficits of autistic children," *Child Development* (1961), 32:437–456.

Because they indicate what operants are likely to be necessary in order to bring about certain events, the discriminative stimuli in a situation are likely to determine, or at least affect, what operants an individual will (4)______________ (*elicit* or *emit*?).

The operants that an individual will tend to emit in a situation are those operants that have in the past been followed by (5)______________ consequences for him.

What will be a reinforcing consequence for me may not be a reinforcing consequence for you. What is a reinforcing consequence for me at one time may not be a (6)______________ for me at other times.

When I want a cup of coffee, for instance, getting a cup of coffee with cream from a vending machine is a reinforcing consequence of my adjusting the vending machine a certain way and inserting a (7)______________.

My wife or sons, however, would want their dimes back were they to get cups of coffee with cream. My wife happens to prefer her coffee black. Our sons prefer hot chocolate or soft drinks. The labels on a vending machine are not intended to act as conditioned stimuli. They are intended to be (8)______________ stimuli that will tell the customer what to do in order to get what he wants.

Individuals must learn to be guided by discriminative stimuli. S^Ds are no more likely to produce or influence a newborn baby's operant response than CSs are likely to elicit (9)__________ responses from it.

A baby does not immediately discriminate between (that is, does not respond discriminatively to) bed post, blanket, bottle, and breast. It takes at least several weeks, in fact, before a baby begins to emit (10)__________ (*operants* or *respondents*?) at the sight of bottle and/or breast that it does not emit just as frequently at other times.

At two or three years of age (or even older), furthermore, it is sometimes a source of amusement or embarrassment to the parents that a child will often call all men (11)__________.

When Daddy (or anyone else!) is driving along the highway or through the city streets, it is quite important that he discriminate where he is and operate the car accordingly. Stop signs, turn signals, mileage signs, horns, sirens, road conditions, traffic signals, pedestrians, other cars, the way his car responds when he turns or puts on the brakes, all of these are among the (12)__________ stimuli to which a good driver responds.

A good driver quickly responds to many different discriminative stimuli and makes the right responses at the right time. Many of these responses are completely automatic for the experienced driver. We even say that they are "reflex." They do not, however, have unconditioned stimuli and they can usually be done in more than one way. They are, therefore, definitely (13)______________ (*operant* or *respondent*?) no matter how automatic they may become.

Regardless of how automatic an operant may become, it still is operant. Operants *never* become (14)____________.

BOOK TITLES AS DISCRIMINATIVE STIMULI

The "Little Blue Books" (an early kind of paperback) once published a number of pairs of volumes in which the same book was put out for sale under two different titles. The object was to see how much the book title would influence sales and which title would sell the best. Here are some of the pairs of titles that were compared. In each pair exactly the same book was sold, except for the change in title.

In each of the following pairs of titles, which title gives the most information about the contents of the book?

Title A	Title B	Gives Most Information
Art of Controversy	How to Argue Logically	(15)________
Markheim	Markheim's Murder	(16)________
Ten O'Clock	What Art Should Mean to You	(17)________

The title that gives the most information about the book is the clearest (18)____________ (*conditioned* or *discriminative*?) stimulus for the possible buyer.

In each pair of titles one of the titles sold at least four times as many copies per year as the other title. (E. Haldeman-Julius, *The First Hundred Million*, New York, Simon & Schuster, 1928). Which title would you predict would sell the most copies in each pair?

Title A	Title B	Will Sell Most Copies
Art of Controversy	How to Argue Logically	(19)________

Markheim	Markheim's Murder	(20)________
Ten O'Clock	What Art Should Mean to You	(21)________

The actual sales reported are: (19) A, less than 1000; B, 30,000. (20) A, less than 1000; B, 7,000. (21) A, 2,000; B, 9,000. It seems that the titles that were clear discriminative stimuli sold (22)____________ (*less* or *more*?) copies.

COGNITIVE STIMULI AND DISCRIMINATIVE STIMULI

The sound of speech and the sight of a book title are stimuli to which a person educated in the language being used *is able to* respond. This makes them (23)____________ (*experimenters' stimuli, proper stimuli,* or *stimulus-actions*?).

Stimuli to which an individual is able to respond are proper stimuli for him. If he also tells us what he is responding to, the stimuli are also (24)____________ (*cognitive* or *discriminative*?) stimuli.

Cognitive stimuli, according to the definition in this book, are stimuli to which an individual (25)__________ (*knows* or *says*?) he is responding.

Sometimes a person says that he does not know why he thinks that there is something wrong with a motor, or that another person is frightened, or that something in a room has changed. Yet though the stimulus (or stimuli) is thus not a cognitive stimulus, the person turns out to be correct! A stimulus does not have to be a cognitive stimulus in order to be a (26)____________-action.

A stimulus does not have to be a cognitive stimulus in order to be a stimulus-action. It does not have to be a cognitive stimulus in order to be a (27)__________ (*conditioned* or *discriminative*?) stimulus for a respondent.

A stimulus does not have to be a cognitive stimulus in order to be CS for a respondent; neither does it have to be a cognitive stimulus in order to be a (28)__________ stimulus for an operant.

S^Ds AND CSs

We learn discriminative stimuli for some responses and we learn conditioned stimuli for other responses. The same stimulus-action, however, may be both CS and S^D. For which of the following responses could a brief written message be a *conditioned* stimulus and for which could it be a *discriminative* stimulus?

Blushing (29)__________

Fear (30)____________

Playing a hand of bridge (31)____________

Solving a mathematics problem (32)____________

Sweating (33)____________

As we have defined conditioned stimuli only respondents (such as blushing, fear, and sweating) are controlled by CSs and only operants (such as playing a hand of cards or solving a mathematics problem) have S^Ds.

DIFFERENT SIMULTANEOUS FUNCTIONS OF THE SAME STIMULUS: AN EXAMPLE

Imagine that the sound of a bell is always followed by an electric shock to your arm unless you press a button when you hear the bell. If you press the button just as soon as you hear the bell, the bell stops and you are not shocked. The shock is fairly severe. Your heart beats faster every time you hear the bell. You quickly learn to press the button each time you hear the bell.

Your heart beating faster is (34)____________ (*operant* or *respondent*?). Pressing the button is (35)____________ (*operant* or *respondent*?).

Heart beating faster is respondent; pressing a button is operant. The fact that the ringing of the bell makes your heart beat faster shows that the ringing of the bell is (36)____________ (*CS* or S^D?) for you.

When you press the button, the bell stops ringing. The ending of the ringing is a (37)____________ consequence of button pressing.

An agent that we want to stop or end, something whose ending is reinforcing to us, is usually something that is aversive or unpleasant. An agent whose termination or ending immediately after an operant is a reinforcing consequence for that operant is a (38)____________ (*positive* or *negative*?) reinforcer.

Nothing happens when you press the button unless you press it when the bell is ringing. If you press the button when the bell is ringing, a reinforcing consequence results (the bell stops ringing and you avoid the shock). Because the ringing of the bell indicates when button pressing will be reinforced, the ringing of the bell is also called (39)____________ (CS or S^D?).

As we see from this example, the same stimulus can affect an individual in several ways at the same time. In this example, the ringing of the bell is CS (*item* 36), a negative reinforcer (*item* 38), and S^D (*item* 39).

BACK TO THE CAT AND THE STOVE LID

"A cat that happens to jump onto a hot stove lid is not likely ever to do so again. In fact this cat may become emotionally upset in the future whenever it even sees a stove lid."

In this quotation, jumping upon the stove lid is (40)__________ (*operant* or *respondent*?). Emotional upset is (41)__________ (*operant* or *respondent*?).

Learning to fear stove lids is (42)__________ (*operant conditioning* or *respondent conditioning*?). Learning to get away from stove lids is (43)__________ (*operant conditioning* or *respondent conditioning*?).

Answer from this list: CS; negative reinforcer; S^D; UCS. Use each answer once in the following four items:

The conditioning of the fear of stove lids is *respondent conditioning*. *In this conditioning*:

Having feet burned (44)__________

Sight of the stove lid (45)__________

The conditioning of the tendency to avoid lids is *operant conditioning. In this conditioning*:

Having feet burned (46)_____________

Sight of the stove lid (47)_____________

RESPONDENT CONDITIONING: The burn of the stove lid unconditionally elicits emotional upset. The sight of the stove lid becomes CS for emotional upset (fear) after it is associated with emotional upset.

OPERANT CONDITIONING: Termination of the heat is a reinforcing consequence of jumping off of the stove. The burn of the stove lid is therefore a negative reinforcer. Sight of the stove indicates that jumping one way will bring it nearer while running in another direction will mean getting away from it. Sight of the stove lid is therefore an S^D for these operants.

NOTES:

1. *Discriminative stimulus* is sometimes defined so that it is possible to refer to an S^D for a respondent. This makes "discriminative stimulus" mean the same thing as "stimulus-action" in our definitions. In practice the term discriminative stimulus is most often used as it is defined and used in these lessons ("a stimulus that indicates what events are likely to follow what operants").

2. B. F. Skinner feels that we use force and punishment far too much. In his novel *Walden Two* (New York: Macmillan, 1948), Skinner describes a society whose culture does not permit the use of any force, coercion, or punishment. The government governs by use of positive reinforcers. In *Walden Two* there is a maximum respect for each individual, and no one can force anyone else to do anything or punish anyone else for not doing or for doing. People work together in order to get what they all want, or one person provides what another person wants in order that he, in turn, may get what he wants. Supply and demand determine the value of all things and of all labor. (Look at the *Columbia Jester* drawing.)

Skinner's *Walden Two* makes an interesting contrast to George Orwell's *1984* (where people are controlled primarily by fear and punishment) and Aldous Huxley's *Brave New World* (New York: Bantam, 1953), where people are controlled primarily by the effects of childhood respondent conditioning.

LESSON TEST: AFTER YOU HAVE COMPLETED THIS LESSON, ANSWER THE FOLLOWING QUESTIONS WITHOUT LOOKING BACK AT THE LESSON:

1. What are the two main differences between operants and respondents?

2. What is the difference between operant conditioning and respondent conditioning?

3. What does it mean when we say that a stimulus is acting as a discriminative stimulus for an individual? What does it mean when we say that a stimulus is a conditioned stimulus-action for an individual?

BEFORE YOU GO ON TO MORE ADVANCED LESSONS IT IS QUITE IMPORTANT THAT YOU UNDERSTAND THESE DISTINCTIONS. CAREFULLY CHECK YOUR ANSWER TO NUMBER 1 BY TURNING BACK TO THE LAST PAGE OF LESSON 4. CHECK ANSWERS TO 2 AND 3 BY LOOKING BACK AT THE LAST TWO PAGES OF LESSON 7. (OR YOU MAY ALSO CHECK YOURSELF BY REFERRING BACK TO THE LIST OF MAJOR CONCEPTS AT THE BEGINNING OF THE BOOK.) CAREFULLY CORRECT EVERY MISTAKE OR OMISSION.

PART IV

A Theory

LESSON 9

Operant Shaping

[Estimated time: 40 minutes]

> Most people are capable of learning and recognizing simple melodies, and equally capable of recognizing the sound of various instruments—but few mortals share the privilege of 'absolute pitch', of being able to identify single notes. In other words, retention of a pattern of stimuli is the rule, retention of an isolated stimulus the exception.
>
> —ARTHUR KOESTLER[1]

In learning any skill, what must be acquired is not an association or any series of associations, but many thousands of associations that will connect specific movements with specific situations. One lesson or one trial is all that is necessary to learn to depress the brake pedal on a car. Learning to drive the car requires a varied experience which will cause the pedal to be depressed in many situations and left severely alone in many others.

—E. R. GUTHRIE[2]

1 *The Act of Creation* (New York: Macmillan, 1964), p. 521.

2 "Conditioning: A Theory of Learning in Terms of Stimulus, Response, and Association," *The Psychology of Learning, Yearbook XLI, Part II* (Chicago: National Society for the Study of Education, 1942), p. 36.

I. P. Pavlov did his earlier work on the processes of digestion and the nervous system (for which he received the Nobel prize in physiology in 1904). Pavlov, however, is now most famous for his experiments involving conditioning of the salivary responses of (1)____________ (*dogs* or *humans*?).

Pavlov's work with respondent conditioning was entirely with the salivary glands of dogs. We quoted him at the beginning of Lesson 5 and briefly discussed his work at the beginning of Project II.

V. M. Bekhterev was a Russian neuropathologist, who spent some time studying with German and French psychologists and psychiatrists. In psychology, Bekhterev is most famous for his studies in the conditioning of defensive muscular reactions in dogs and men.

These two men, (2)__________ and (3)__________, are the pioneers of work with conditioning.

Pavlov receives credit for preceding Bekhterev in investigating respondent conditioning. Therefore, respondent conditioning is sometimes called (4)__________ian conditioning.

Pavlov used a simple respondent, *salivation*, as the response to be associated with new stimuli. Bekhterev investigated a muscular response: *flexion of the foreleg and retraction of the foot* when electric shock is applied to the foot. Bekhterev's unit of response seems to fall somewhere between being respondent and being (5)__________.

Whether a particular type of response should be classified as operant or as respondent is not always very clear. Bekhterev's experiments have usually been described as studies of respondent conditioning. Bekhterev used almost exactly the same procedures that (6)__________ used.

Bekhterev also obtained the same sort of results: a stimulus that would not initially affect a certain response began to elicit this response after it had occurred in the experimental situation at the same time as the (7)________ (*response* or *stimulus*?) on a number of occasions.

But the response used by Pavlov in his studies was salivation, whereas the response studied by Bekhterev was (8)__________.

The foot-withdrawal response *seems* to be a simple, consistent, and automatic response that the individual does not need to learn how to make. Electric shock applied to the foot seems to be (9)__________ (*CS* or *UCS*?) for foot-withdrawal.

At the first application of electric shock to the foot, however, the records of experimenters using Bekhterev's techniques indicate that a violent jerking occurs that may even temporarily press the foot more firmly against the source of the (10)_______________.

Only after several shocks does the response become a clear, clean withdrawal response. This is important because it is (11)_______________, *not respondents*, that "change in form and can be done in several different ways."

Operants, *not* respondents, become more efficient with practice. Apparently the individual must (12)_____________ how to terminate or reduce a "painful" stimulus by withdrawing.

Apparently Bekhterev's dogs had to learn to make a clear, clean response, and the exact form of the withdrawal response could be further modified in various somewhat different situations. Thus, according to our definitions, we must classify foot-withdrawal as (13)__________.

If foot-withdrawal is operant, it may become completely automatic, but it can never stop being operant and become (14)_______________.

Examined in detail, foot-withdrawal is not a simple response at all but a complex combination of contraction of many individual flexor muscles in the leg without the contraction of many individual extensor muscles. The simple basic response that would seem most nearly to correspond to secretion of saliva by a single salivary gland is the contraction of a single (15)____________.

Contraction of a single muscle is a response for which there are unconditioned stimuli. Contraction of a single muscle is a response that does not change in form and can be done in only one way. Contraction of a single muscle is a response that usually cannot be controlled by specific instructions or commands. Thus it would seem that contraction of a single muscle is (16)____________.

MUSCLE CONTRACTION, MOVEMENT, AND OPERANT

Contraction of a single muscle is respondent. These respondents, however, are somewhat different from other respondents. Contraction of a muscle creates stimuli that may be UCS or CS for (17)__________ of other muscles.

Contraction of a muscle creates stimuli that may be UCS or CS for contraction of other muscles. There are receptors, called "proprioceptors" (sensory structures similar in function to the eye and ear), which are located in muscles, joints, tendons, and in the inner ear. These receptors, called (18)____________, are sensitive to movements of our own bodies.

The proprioceptors make coordination possible between what is happening in one part of the body and what is going on elsewhere in the body. *Muscle contractions tend to occur in patterns even in the newborn infant. These patterns are often modified* during the life of an individual. Therefore, these patterns of muscle contraction are (19)____________ (*operant* or *respondent*?).

Operants are combination and coordinations of muscle contractions. Each separate individual muscle contraction, however, is a (20)____________.

Contraction of a separate individual muscle is respondent. *At least theoretically* we could discover and identify the stimulus for every contraction or (21)____________ment of a muscle.

Movement designates a *relationship* between a *specific stimulus and a muscular contraction* that immediately follows this stimulus. *Operant* designates a relationship between a *coordination of movements* and some *change* in the environment that *they produce*. Operants are actions involving many individual (22)____________.

The movements or muscle contractions involved in opening a door with the right hand and opening it with the left hand are completely different; yet the effect is the same and the name for the response is the same if the response we are naming is the total (23)__________ (*operant* or *respondent*?), regardless of how it is done.

Operants are *named* in terms of *what is done*, such as running away, attacking, opening a door, writing a letter, or pressing a lever. The outcome or effect is named. In most cases the outcome or effect in different circumstances can be achieved by the individual making many different combinations of (24)__________.

OPERANT SHAPING

Each separate movement or muscle contraction is respondent. An operant consists of many such movements. Operants, however, never become respondents and respondents never become (25)__________.

Operants are not made up of respondent muscle twitches in the way that a house is built of sticks and stones. The general and massive operant patterns of movement of the whole body of the infant are modified by the environment as the infant grows. Precise operants develop both as a result of biological maturation and as the behavior of the infant is gradually modified by the environment in somewhat the same way that a piece of (26)__________ is modified by an artist making a statue.

The piece of stone or other material that he uses limits and guides the artist by its hardness, size, form, and so forth. The sculptor cuts away large areas to give the stone a certain general form. Then finer and finer details are shaped. (27)____________ responses often develop in somewhat the same way.

Operants can theoretically be analyzed into complex interactions of UCSs, CSs, and respondent muscle contractions. Operants, however, (28)____________ (*are* or *are not*?) built up of muscle contractions in the way that a house may be built of sticks and stones.

Operants are not usually built up by combining individual muscle contractions. They are shaped out from living, growing, internally determined, initial patterns and coordinations of movements.

DEFINITION: Operant shaping *is the development of new operant-sequences as a result of interaction of a particular kind of individual with a particular kind of environment.*

Operant shaping is the development of new (29)_________.

Operant shaping is the development of new operant-sequences as a result of interaction of a particular kind of individual with a particular kind of environment. This may involve (a) change in the exact pattern and sequence of muscle contractions; (b) increase in the number and exactness of behavioral situations which will produce the operant and in the number of different combinations of individual muscle contractions that will occur in slightly different situations to bring about the same sort of consequence; (c) increase in the number of movements coordinated together so that they tend to occur or not to occur as a set or sequence. (This third type is sometimes called *operant chaining.*)

Shaping changes the form of the operant. Shaping is much more complex than conditioning. As we have defined operant conditioning and respondent conditioning, (30)______________ (*both types* or *neither type*?) of conditioning change(s) the form of the response being conditioned.

It must now be stressed, if it was not clear before, that *neither operant* conditioning nor *respondent* conditioning changes the form of the response being conditioned. Respondent conditioning is defined as (31)_________. (Give the entire definition on the back of your answer sheet.)

Respondent conditioning is the name for the process by which a stimulus becomes conditioned to elicit a respondent by being associated with that respondent. Operant conditioning is defined as (32)______________. (Give the entire definition on the back of your answer sheet.)

Operant conditioning is the name for the process by which a behavioral situation comes to produce a certain type of operant more and more frequently when such operants are followed by reinforcing consequences. *Operant shaping* usually consists of a combination of respondent conditioning and operant conditioning so that one part of a response becomes a cue for further parts, and so forth.

Few psychologists would object to the definition of respondent conditioning and operant conditioning as given in this book. The proposition that individual movements are respondent, however, has not been specifically developed in any other book (so far as the author is aware). This proposition is a deduction from Guthrie's contiguity theory of learning. We shall discuss the relationship of operant and respondent conditioning again after we study some lessons explaining Guthrie's theory.

OBSERVATION OF A BABY

In the following lengthy quotation, John B. Watson describes his careful observation of the interaction of learning and maturation during the shaping of two operants. One might think that a child automatically and naturally reaches for candy and just as naturally pulls its hand away from being burned by a candle. Instead we find that a child is several months old before it can learn how to reach for and grasp objects such as candy. *Avoidance responses develop even later*! When the baby Watson is observing is five months of age, a burn from a candle flame immediately elicits flexion of the baby's fingers. It takes several burns, however, before she learns to withdraw her hand. She is two months older before she has developed further and learned not to reach out and burn herself in the candle flame.

Systematic tests were begun upon L on the 80th day. She was carefully tested each week thereafter in such a way that progress in eye-hand coordination could be observed. . . . After dangling the candy for a minute or two it was put into her mouth by the experimenter if she failed to reach for it.

. . . . .

Age, 101 days. . . . She failed to reach for the candy on five presentations. . . .

. . . . .

115 days. Not much further advance in reaching. . . .

. . . . .

129 days. . . . Followed it with her eyes and when it was six inches distant from her face, she struck the candy with the back of her hand in two seconds, then pushed it over to the other hand, then to her chin, finally worrying it into her mouth. . . .

136 days. . . . The right hand started up immediately, grasped the candy and carried it to the mouth. Time, 8 seconds. . . .

. . . . .

Reaching for the Candle. —While the tests on reaching for candy were being conducted she was tried frequently with an ordinary lighted wax candle. She was tested first on the 150th day (reaching for candy had been established, see above). The room was darkened. She reached immediately with the right hand, advancing the whole upper part of the body. She then held out both hands, reaching as far out from her mother's lap as possible. Heat did not seem to make her withdraw even when the flame was held as close to her hand as an eighth of an inch. . . . On the last three trials her hand was allowed to touch the flame, causing flexion of the fingers, but this did not deter her from reaching. On the succeeding trial she reached immediately with the right hand, the flame touching the fingers and again causing flexion. The definite withdrawal of the whole hand occurred sharply on this trial, but the child did not cry. Twenty-five trials in all were given. In most cases the hand was allowed to come close enough to cause flexion of the fingers.

. . . . .

164 days. A similar set of tests was given. She would reach continually for the candle, regardless of the fact that her fingers were often scorched.

. . . . .

178 days. Definite progress in avoidance was noted.

. . . . .

We have carried out similar tests both on reaching for candy and for the candle upon several children (at least fifteen) with results wholly similar to the above. . . .

—JOHN B. WATSON[3]

REVIEW

a. The first man to study respondent conditioning was (33)____________.

b. The kind of response that does not change in form is called (34)____________.

[3] *Psychology from the Standpoint of a Behaviorist* (Philadelphia: Lippincott, 1919), pp. 275–280.

c. The kind of learning in which the form of response changes is called (35)_______________.

d. The evidence that Watson gathered is an early example demonstrating the fact that the withdrawal response is (36)_______________ (*operant* or *respondent*?).

e. The process of development of a clean consistent foot-withdrawal response by the dogs Bekhterev studied and the development of avoidance of the candle by the babies Watson studied are examples of operant (37)_______________ (*conditioning* or *shaping*?).

f. Operants (38)_______________ (*are* or *are not*?) built up of respondent muscle contractions in the way that a house is built of sticks and stones.

(The answers to the review questions are: 33, Pavlov; 34, respondent; 35, operant shaping; 36, operant; 37, operant shaping; 38, are not.)

LESSON TEST: AFTER YOU HAVE COMPLETED THIS LESSON, ANSWER THE FOLLOWING QUESTIONS WITHOUT LOOKING BACK AT THE LESSON:

1. What was the main difference between the kind of conditioning studied by Pavlov and the kind studied by Bekhterev?

2. What is the difference between a movement and an operant?

3. Briefly define operant shaping.

4. What are the two operants described by Watson in the long quotation in this lesson? At what age was the shaping of each of these operants fairly complete?

5. Give an example of operant shaping of human behavior in elementary schools. Describe the behavior as it is before shaping, the kind of reinforcers used, and what the final operant-sequence is.

CHECK YOUR ANSWERS (OR EXCHANGE ANSWERS AND CHECK) BY LOOKING BACK AT THE LESSON. CAREFULLY CORRECT EVERY MISTAKE OR OMISSION.

LESSON

10

Contiguity

[Estimated time: 25 minutes]

How do you suppose I know about all these things that took place so long ago?

I don't.

I'm only guessing about them.

But there are different kinds of guesses. If I hold out my two closed hands and ask you to guess which one has the penny in it, that is one kind of guess. Your guess might be right or it might be wrong. It would be just your luck.

But there is another kind of guess. When there is snow on the ground and I see tracks of a boot in the snow, I guess that a man must have passed by, for boots don't usually walk without someone in them. That kind of guess is just not luck. . . .

—V. M. HILLYER[1]

Scientists often make the second kind of guess. They call these guesses "hypotheses" and "theories." The theory of learning that we shall study in these lessons is the *contiguity* (1)______________ of E. R. Guthrie.

1 *A Child's History of the World* (New York: Appleton-Century-Crofts, 1951), p. 10.

Guthrie's contiguity theory of learning is not the only theory of how (2)____________ occurs.

Guthrie's theory is one of the oldest theories of how learning occurs. In some ways it is the (3)____________ (*simplest* or *most complex*?) theory, and this makes it easier for students to understand.

We have chosen to study and develop one form of E. R. (4)____________'s contiguity theory in these lessons.

In this lesson we shall study three of the basic principles of Guthrie's (5)____________ (*contiguity* or *continuity*?) theory.

Contiguity means "closeness" or "nearness." *Contiguous* is a synonym for "close" or (6)"____________."

Events that are contiguous in time are events that happen at about the same (7)____________.

Events that happen at about the same time tend to be associated. This principle has a very long history in philosophy and psychology. For instance, the pre-Christian Greek scholar Aristotle observed and described the principle of (8)____________ (*association* or *conditioning*?) by contiguity in time.

Association of ideas rather than conditioning of stimulus-actions to respondents was the concern of famous philosopher-psychologists of the past such as Aristotle, Berkeley, Hume, James Mill, Bain, Hartley, and William James. The general rule, however, has not changed: association tends to result between events that happen at about the same (9)____________.

We shall study E. R. (10)____________'s more recent version of this ancient theory.

Guthrie's theory is called the (11)____________ theory of learning.

According to Guthrie's theory, a stimulus-action becomes conditioned to all of the (12)____________ (*ideas* or *responses*?) that are associated with it by occurring at the same time.

We have already learned that a stimulus-action becomes CS for a respondent by occurring at a time when another stimulus-action happens to be eliciting that respondent. But according to Guthrie this contiguity in time between stimulus and response that results in conditioning needs to happen only once!

PRINCIPLE A: RESPONDENT CONDITIONING

Conditioning requires only one *association. Every stimulus-action immediately and completely becomes* CS *for* all *of the respondents elicited from the individual by the other stimulus-actions in the behavioral situation at that time.*

According to Principle A, every stimulus-action immediately and (13)____________ becomes conditioned to all of the respondents that occur at the same time as the response to the stimulus-action.

A stimulus-action needs to accompany a respondent (14)____________ (*more than once* or *only once*?) in order to become CS for that respondent.

After it is associated with a different respondent, UCS for one respondent also becomes (15)____________ (*CS* or *UCS*?) for the different respondent.

In order to become CS for the respondent, a stimulus-action needs to accompany that respondent only once. The stimulus-action does not stop being UCS for its natural respondent, and a stimulus-action may be CS for (16)____________ (*many different respondents* or *only one respondent*?) at the same time.

A stimulus-action becomes CS for a respondent by the kind of learning called (17)____________ conditioning.

PRINCIPLE A: RESPONDENT CONDITIONING states that conditioning requires only (18)____________ association. Every (19)____________ (*stimulus-action* or *experimenter's stimulus*?) immediately and completely becomes (20)____________ (*CS* or *UCS*?) for all of the respondents elicited from the individual by the other stimulus-actions in the (21)____________ (*behavioral* or *physical*?) situation at that time.

PRINCIPLE A: RESPONDENT CONDITIONING states that conditioning requires only one association. Every stimulus-action immediately and completely becomes CS for all of the respondents elicited by the other stimulus-actions in the behavioral situation at that time.

Principle A says that respondent conditioning requires only *one association*. Yet both Pavlov's dogs and students learning to "eat fire" (Project II) usually seem to require several associations before respondent conditioning is evident. Principles B and C explain why respondent conditioning *seems* to require more than one association.

PRINCIPLE B: DYNAMIC SITUATIONS

An individual is not likely ever to be in exactly the same total behavioral situation twice in his life.

Situations constantly change because the organism changes (becomes larger, becomes older, changes in many different ways at different times), because the stimuli from inside the organism change (for example, stimuli from the muscles and stomach), because stimuli from outside the organism change (for example, noises and smells), and because the combinations, groupings, and patterns of stimulus-action change.

The word "dynamic" means "changing." Behavioral situations are almost always (22)____________ (*dynamic* or *static*?) situations.

The total (23)____________ situation of an individual is almost always *dynamic*.

An individual may respond to the same stimulus-action many times, but an individual (24)____________ (*is* or *is not*?) likely to be in exactly the same total behavioral situation twice in his life.

Behavioral situations constantly change. Behavioral situations are never static; they are always (25)________(which means "*changing*").

PRINCIPLE B: DYNAMIC (26)____________. An individual is not likely ever to be in exactly the same total behavioral situation twice in his life.

PRINCIPLE C: RESPONSE PROBABILITY

When there is no UCS acting to elicit or to stop the respondent, the more stimulus-actions in the behavioral situation at that time that are CS for that respondent, the more likely the behavioral situation will elicit that respondent from the individual.

Probability means "closeness to certainty." Something that is probable is something that is expected to happen but might not happen. The higher the probability of something happening, the (27)__________ (*less* or *more*?) certain it is to happen.

For example, the more stimulus-actions in the behavioral situation *that are* CS for that respondent, the (28)____________ (*less* or *more*?) likely the behavioral situation will elicit that respondent.

When there is no UCS acting to elicit or to stop the respondent, a behavioral situation is more likely to elicit that respondent the more stimulus-actions that are *in the behavioral situation* at that time that are (29)__________ for that respondent.

We often *say* that one CS elicits the respondent, but *no one stimulus* by itself is the total cause of any response. Even a (30)__________ (*CS* or *UCS*?) for a respondent may not elicit that respondent.

For example, a bright light shining in your eyes is UCS for contraction of your eye pupils. However, your eye pupils will not (31)__________ if you have recently swallowed certain medicines.

The medicine has changed the total (32)__________ situation.

Principle A says that every stimulus-action in the behavioral situation of the individual at the time will immediately and completely become (33)__________ for all of the respondents elicited by the other stimulus-actions at that time.

An individual, however, may never be in exactly or even nearly the same total behavioral situation twice in his life because behavioral situations are (34)__________.

This is why we need Principle C, the principle of (35)______________ probability.

Response probability is very (36)______________ (*high* or *low*?) for a respondent when the UCS for this respondent occurs.

How high the probability will be depends on the rest of the (37)______________ situation.

In a behavioral situation in which there is no UCS acting to stop the respondent and also no UCS acting to elicit the respondent, the probability of the response will depend upon how many of the stimulus-actions in the behavioral situation are (38)______________ for that respondent.

How many of the stimulus-actions *in the behavioral situation at that time are CS for that respondent* will determine whether or not that respondent will be elicited if there is no UCS acting to elicit or to (39)______________ the respondent.

PRINCIPLE C: RESPONSE PROBABILITY. When there is no UCS acting to elicit or to stop the respondent, the more stimulus-actions in the behavioral situation at that time that are (40)______________ for that respondent, the more likely the (41)______________ situation will elicit that respondent from the individual.

PRINCIPLE C: RESPONSE PROBABILITY. When there is no UCS acting to elicit or to stop the respondent, the more stimulus-actions in the behavioral situation at that time that are CS for that respondent, the more likely the behavioral situation will elicit that respondent from the individual.

REVIEW

In this lesson, we have studied three of the principles basic to E. R. (42)____________'s theory of learning.

Guthrie's theory of learning is named the (43)________ theory of learning.

Contiguity means "nearness" or "closeness." According to Guthrie's theory there must be contiguity in time *between stimulus-action and* (44)__________ in order for learning to occur.

Complete conditioning of a response to the entire behavioral situation requires how many associations? (45)____________

Only one association is required for conditioning to the entire behavioral situation. The individual may never, however, be in exactly the same behavioral situation again because behavioral situations are (46)__________.

Because behavioral situations are dynamic, we need a principle of response probability. The principle of response probability says that when there is no UCS acting to elicit or to stop the respondent, the more (47)__________ (*CSs* or *CSs for that respondent?*) present, the more likely the behavioral situation will elicit that respondent.

We are not studying Guthrie's theory exactly as he formulated it. These lessons present a further revision of Virginia Voeks' analysis of Guthrie's theory ("Formalization and clarification of a theory of learning," *J. Psychol.* [1950], *30*:341–362).

LESSON TEST: AFTER YOU HAVE COMPLETED THIS LESSON, ANSWER THE FOLLOWING QUESTIONS WITHOUT LOOKING BACK AT THE LESSON:

1. We are studying a revision of Virginia __________, analysis of Guthrie's theory.
2. The principle of *respondent conditioning* says that conditioning requires only *one* association. That every stimulus-action __________.
3. The principle of dynamic situations says that an individual __________.
4. The principle of response probability says that if there is no UCS acting to __________ or to __________ the respondent, __________ the more likely the behavioral situation will elicit that respondent.
5. According to the contiguity theory *one* association is all that is needed for complete conditioning. How does the

theory explain the fact that conditioning actually *almost always seems to take* many associations?

CHECK YOUR ANSWERS (OR EXCHANGE ANSWERS AND CHECK) BY LOOKING BACK AT THE LESSON. CAREFULLY CORRECT EVERY MISTAKE OR OMISSION.

LESSON

11

Permanency of Conditioning

[Estimated time: 30 minutes]

The Hell, to be endured hereafter, of which theology tells, is no worse than the hell we make for ourselves in this world by habitually fashioning our characters in the wrong way. Could the young but realize how soon they will become mere walking bundles of habits, they would give more heed to their conduct while in the plastic state. We are spinning our own fates, good or evil, and never to be undone. Every smallest stroke of virtue or of vice leaves its never so little scar. The drunken Rip Van Winkle, in Jefferson's play, excuses himself for every fresh dereliction by saying, 'I won't count this time!' Well! He may not count it, and a kind Heaven may not count it; but it is being counted none the less. Down among his nerve cells and fibres the molecules are counting it, registering and storing it up to be used against him when the next temptation comes. Nothing we ever do is, in strict scientific literalness, wiped out. Of course this has its good side as well as its bad one. As we become permanent drunkards by so many separate drinks, we become saints in the moral, and authorities and experts in the practical and scientific spheres, by so many separate acts and hours of work.

—WILLIAM JAMES[1]

[1] *Psychology* (Cleveland: World, 1948), pp. 149–150.

In Lesson 10 we studied three of the principles of Guthrie's (1)____________ theory of learning.

Principle A says that stimulus-actions must be associated with respondents (2)____________ (*many times* or *only once*?) in order to be completely conditioned to these respondents.

Principle B is the principle that behavioral situations are (3)____________.

Every time a respondent occurs, it occurs in at least a slightly different (4)____________ situation.

Any stimulus-action in the behavioral situation that was not a stimulus-action for the respondent becomes (5)____________ for that respondent, according to *Principle A*.

A CS for a respondent is a stimulus-action that became a CS for that respondent by being conditioned to that respondent.

Respondent *One* is elicited from S ten different times in the experimental room. Respondent *Two* is elicited from S three different times in the experimental room. Which respondent will have gained the most CSs? (6)__________

Conditioning happens immediately and completely all at one time (*Principle A*), but behavioral situations are dynamic (*Principle B*). The more different behavioral situations are associated with the respondent, the more (7)______________ (*CSs, S^D^s, or UCSs?*) the respondent will have.

The more CSs for the respondent there are in a behavioral situation, the more likely (more probable) the behavioral situation will elicit the respondent if there is no (8)______________ stimulus acting to elicit or to stop that respondent.

When there is no UCS acting to elicit or to stop the respondent, the behavioral situation is more likely to elicit that respondent if there are more stimulus-actions in the behavioral situation which are CS for that respondent. This is *Principle C*, the principle of response (9)______________ (*conditioned* or *probability*?).

The probability that the respondent will happen is greater when more CSs for that respondent are in the situation.

In Project II you learned how to condition a behavioral situation which elicted one respondent so that it would elicit the opposite respondent. You were instructed to hold the flame far away at first and then gradually to bring it closer, being careful never to bring it closer so fast that your mouth would dry up. *The purpose of these instructions was to keep the behavioral situation changing so slowly that the flame would never make your mouth dry up and more and more situations containing the flame closer and closer to you would be conditioned to normal salivation.*

PRINCIPLE D: CONDITIONED STIMULI

The conditioned stimulus-action usually is a group or pattern of several proper stimuli.

A "stimulus-action" upon an individual is an (10)________ (*event* or *agent*?) that (11)________ (*does* or *does not*?) elicit or change a response by that individual.

A stimulus-action upon an individual is an *event* that *does* elicit or change a response by that individual. A proper stimulus is an event that (12)____________ elicit or change a response by that individual.

A proper stimulus is an event that *is able to* elicit or change a response by that individual. Every proper stimulus that occurs is not necessarily a (13)____________ upon that individual.

A proper stimulus is not necessarily a stimulus-action. At the time it does elicit or change a response, an event is called a stimulus-action. An event is not a stimulus-action if it is not eliciting or changing some (14)__________.

If a certain response is produced by a grouping or pattern of three or four proper stimuli, then the occurrence of this group or pattern of stimuli is the event that is the (15)__________ for this response.

A stimulus-action is an event that affects an individual. A stimulus-action may be very simple, such as a change in one stimulus-agent. A stimulus-action may be very complex, such as the occurrence of a particular grouping or pattern of several (16)__________.

The occurrence of a particular group of several proper stimuli in a certain pattern may be a stimulus-action. For example, I can respond to the smell of fried fish, to the sight of fried fish, to the smell of fish sauce, to the sight of fish sauce, and to many other sights, sounds, and smells at a dinner party, each as a separate event. However, I may also respond to the fish being served in the sauce at the dinner party as one single event, as one (17)__________.

PRINCIPLE D: CONDITIONED STIMULI. The conditioned stimulus-action usually is a (18)__________ or pattern of several proper stimuli.

PRINCIPLE D: CONDITIONED STIMULI. The conditioned stimulus-action usually is a group or pattern of several proper stimuli.

PRINCIPLE E: PERMANENCY OF CONDITIONING

Conditioning is permanent. The only way that CS for a respondent can stop being CS for that respondent is by conditioning CS to an incompatible respondent.

Incompatible means "not able to happen at the same time." For example, the respondent *salivating more* and the respondent *salivating less* are (19)____________ respondents.

Another example of respondents that are likely to be incompatible to each other is blushing (more blood than usual going to the surface of the skin and making the skin of the face change color) and (20)____________ (which one? (a) *change in skin temperature*; (b) *heart beating more slowly*; (c) *increase in salivation*).

Heart beating more slowly is likely to be an incompatible response to blushing because when your heart beats more slowly you have less blood pressure available to force blood to the surface of your skin when the internal blood vessels are constricted.

Principle E says that conditioning is (21)________.

According to Guthrie's theory, conditioning is permanent. Once a stimulus-action becomes CS for a respondent there is (22)____________ (*more than one way, no way,* or *only one way*?) that it can stop being CS for that respondent.

The only way that CS for a respondent can stop being CS for that respondent is by conditioning CS to an (23)________ respondent.

This is *Principle E*: (24)____________ of Conditioning.

PRINCIPLE E: PERMANENCY OF (25)____________. (26)____________ is permanent. The only way that (27)____________ for a respondent can stop being (28)____________ for that respondent is by conditioning CS to an (29)____________ respondent.

PRINCIPLE E: PERMANENCY OF CONDITIONING. Conditioning is permanent. The only way that CS for a respondent can stop CS for that respondent is by conditioning CS to an incompatible respondent.

RESPONSE EXTINCTION

According to Principle E, conditioning is (30)________.

Does this mean that it can never be changed? (31)________.

No! Principle E says that there is one way that CS for a respondent can stop being CS for that respondent. CS for a respondent can stop being CS for that respondent by being conditioned to an (32)____________ respondent.

When CS is conditioned to an incompatible respondent, the conditioning is certainly changed, but it did not just fade out and disappear. New conditioning replaced old (33)____________.

Conditioning is permanent *unless counterconditioning takes place*. One kind of counterconditioning is caller *response extinction*. Pavlov found that as he associated a bell more and more times with salivation by the dog, more and more groups and patterns of stimulus-action were conditioned to salivation (*Principles A, B, and D*). If, however, he rang the bell many times without putting any acid into the dog's mouth, the bell occurred some times when there were not enough CSs present to elicit salivation without UCS (*Principle C*). Whenever this happened, all of the stimulus-actions were conditioned to *not salivating* (*Principles A and E*).

The more groups and patterns of proper stimuli that include the bell were associated with *not* salivating, the (24)______________ (*less* or *more*?) likely the dog was to salivate the next time he heard the bell.

The more groups and patterns of proper stimuli that include the bell were associated with not salivating, the less likely the dog was to salivate the next time he heard the bell (*Principle C*). This is an example of the kind of counterconditioning called *respondent* (35)______________.

DEFINITION: *Respondent extinction* is the name of the process by which CS for a respondent stops being CS for that respondent by being associated with situations in which the respondent is not elicited (that is, by occurring in situations without UCS).

Respondent extinction is likely to occur when (a) CS is presented many times without UCS, or (b) UCS is presented many times without CS. Which? (36)____________

When CS for a respondent occurs without UCS for that respondent, some other UCS may elicit an incompatible respondent. CS will then be conditioned to the (37)______________ (*first respondent* or *incompatible respondent*?).

The incompatible respondent will be elicited by CS if CS has been associated with it more recently than with the first respondent. (Principle E)

UCS for a respondent may occur without CS as many times as one wishes, but as soon as CS does occur, CS will tend to elicit the respondent CS was associated with the last time CS occurred.

LESSON TEST: AFTER YOU HAVE COMPLETED THIS LESSON, ANSWER THE FOLLOWING QUESTIONS WITHOUT LOOKING BACK AT THE LESSON:

1. Write out the complete principle of *respondent conditioning* (in your own words, if you wish).
2. Write out the complete principle of *response probability* (in your own words, if you wish).
3. Write out the complete principle of *permanency of conditioning*.
4. UCS may occur many times without CS yet no extinction of CS will result. For extinction of a stimulus-action's properties as a CS the CS must ____________.
5. If the conditioned response to CS has been completely extinguished during one training period, when CS is presented the next day, the conditioned response is likely to be elicited by CS again. (This is called "spontaneous recovery" of an extinguished response.) How can the contiguity theory explain this? (Hint: *dynamic situaations* and *response probability*.)

CHECK YOUR ANSWERS (OR EXCHANGE ANSWERS AND CHECK) BY LOOKING BACK AT THE LESSON. CHANGE ANY ANSWERS THAT YOU WISH TO CHANGE. YOU DO NOT NEED TO MEMORIZE THESE PRINCIPLES WORD FOR WORD. IF YOU REALLY UNDERSTAND THEM, HOWEVER, YOU WILL BE ABLE TO STATE EACH PRINCIPLE COMPLETELY IN YOUR OWN WORDS.

LESSON

12

Respondents, Operants, and Contiguity

[Estimated time: 35 minutes]

We can discuss actual behavior only by choosing some nameable detail in which we happen to be interested. The rest we either take for granted or forget. It should always be kept in mind that there is this total response from which the recorded or observed feature is abstracted.

—E. R. GUTHRIE[1]

The first man to experiment with respondent conditioning was Ivan Petrovich (1)____________.

Pavlov was *not* a psychologist. He was an internationally famous (2)____________ (*physiologist* or *physicist*?).

Pavlov was a Russion physiologist. But in the U.S.A. he has had more influence on modern experimental (3)____________ than on physiology.

1 "Conditioning: A Theory of Learning in Terms of Stimulus, Response, and Association," *The Psychology of Learning, Yearbook XLI, Part II* (Chicago: National Society for the Study of Education, 1942), p. 20.

Pavlov arranged his laboratory so that the amount of salivation by a dog *S* could be measured. When a small amount of dilute acid was put into *S*'s mouth, an untrained *S* would salivate. When a bell rang, an untrained *S* (4)______________ (*would* or *would not*?) salivate.

Pavlov found that he could condition the bell for *S* so that *S* would salivate when *S* heard the bell. This was done by ringing the bell just before the (5)______________ was put in *S*'s mouth.

At first the bell did not elicit salivation. The more times the bell rang just before acid, the (6)______________ (*less* or *more*?) *S* salivated when the bell rang.

After about thirty associations between the bell and salivation, *S* salivated about as much to the bell as to the acid. In this study by Pavlov, the sound of the bell was the (7)______________ stimulus, and the acid being put into *S*'s mouth was the (8)______________ stimulus.

The bell was the conditioned stimulus (CS), and the acid in the mouth was the unconditioned stimulus (UCS).

According to Guthrie's theory, "Every stimulus-action immediately and completely becomes CS for all of the respondents elicited by the other stimulus-actions at that time." This is *Principle* (9)____________ (*A*, *B*, *C*, *D*, or or *E*?).

Principle A says "immediately and completely." This means "all at *one* time" not "after about (10)____________ (*five* or *thirty*?) associations." (As Pavlov found!)

"Immediately and completely" means "all at one time" not "after about thirty associations." Also *Principle A* says that "every stimulus-action" becomes CS, not some one stimulus such as the ringing of a (11)____________.

RESPONDENT CONDITIONING

How might Guthrie's theory explain the way the bell gradually began to make *S* salivate more and more? (Or how fire in or near your mouth gradually came to inhibit your salivation less and less in our experimental analysis lesson?) We have studied five basic principles of Guthrie's theory: *A*: *Conditioning*; *B*: *Dynamic Situations*; *C*: *Response Probability*; *D*: *Conditioned Stimuli*; *E*: *Permanency of Conditioning*. For each of the following five paragraphs pick the principle that is particularly important:

1. When the mild acid is put into *S*'s mouth, the acid makes some of the salivary glands in the dog's mouth secrete saliva. Every event to which *S* is responding at

the same time as the salivation becomes CS for salivation by each of these glands.

Principle (12)_______________ (*A* or *B*?)

2. A few minutes later, acid is presented a second time. The physical situation has changed very little. The behavioral situation of the dog, however, may be quite different. This time *S* responds to the bell, *S*'s tongue is in a different position, the collar pulls in a different way, *S* has stopped sniffing and closed his eyes, no insect is biting. *S*'s behavioral situation is now quite different from *S*'s behavioral situation when the acid was put into his mouth before.

Principle (13)_______________ (*B* or *C*?)

3. Every stimulus-action that is associated with salivation becomes CS for salivation, but if a CS for salivation occurs and there is no salivation, the stimulus-action that was CS for salivation will become CS for not salivating.

Principle (14)_______________ (*D* or *E*?)

4. If *S* is responding to bell at the time *S* salivates, the bell becomes CS for salivation. Only those stimuli that are stimulus-actions (either individual proper stimuli for the dog or groups and combinations of proper stimuli responded to as a single stimulus-action) become CS for salivation. The feel of the collar may sometimes be part

of a CS for salivation and at other times part of a CS for not salivating. The feel of the collar whenever the bell is ringing might be CS for salivation, and the feel of the collar whenever the bell is not ringing might be CS for not salivating.

Principle (15)____________ (*C* or *D*?)

5. The more times the bell rings just before and while *S* is salivating, the more groups and patterns of stimulus-action (that each contains the bell) become CS for salivation.

The more CSs for salivation there are in the behavioral situation when the bell rings, the more likely that saliva will be elicited from each of *S*'s salivary glands. The more of the glands that secrete saliva and the longer that they secrete saliva, the more *S*'s mouth will be full of saliva for Pavlov to measure.

Principle (16)____________ (*C* or *E*?)

(Each of the last five answers should have been different and the order of the answers: A, B, E, D, C.)

In Guthrie's own words:

> It is very significant that Pavlov was able to reduce the number of pairings necessary by taking his precautions to limit the variety of the dog's activities in the stand, by

using a soundproof room, by excluding the experimenter from the room, by giving the dog preliminary experience in the apparatus in order that it should struggle less during the experiment. *It appears that practice is necessary to the extent that the response must be elicitable from a variety of situations.* Thus, as practice is continued, the dog acquires many conditioned responses, and a new application of the signal will be the proper component of these practiced associations.

—E. R. GUTHRIE[2]

PRINCIPLE F: CONTIGUITY AND OPERANTS

Any specific operant can be analyzed into a sequence of muscular contractions. Each of these muscular contractions is respondent. Therefore, Principle A can be applied to operants.

Stimuli that control operants by indicating which operants will be followed by reinforcing consequences are called (17)____________ (*conditioned stimuli* or *discriminative stimuli*?).

Stimuli become *discriminative* stimuli for (18)__________ (*operants or respondents*?) that they accompany.

Stimuli become *conditioned* stimuli for (19)__________ (*operants* or *respondents*?) that they accompany.

2 *Op. cit.*, p. 32.

Guthrie applies Principle A to both operants and respondents. As we studied Principle A, we applied it only to respondents. Principle A states: "Conditioning requires only (20)________. Every stimulus-action ________."
(Write out the entire principle on the back of your answer sheet.)

Principle A can be modified to apply to both operants and respondents by using the word "cue" to mean both CS and S^D and changing the principle to read: "Conditioning requires only *one* association. Every stimulus-action immediately and completely becomes a (21)________ (*cue* or *CS*?) for all of the responses of the individual that occur in the behavioral situation at that time."

ASSOCIATIVE LEARNING

Guthrie gives the following example of the Principle of Association by Contiguity in Time applied to an operant behavioral problem that many parents encounter:

> The mother of a ten-year-old girl complained to a psychologist that for two years her daughter had annoyed her by a habit of tossing coat and hat on the floor as she entered the house. On a hundred occasions the mother had insisted that the girl pick up the clothing and hang it in its place. These wild ways were changed only after the mother, on advice, began to insist not that the girl pick up the fallen garments from the floor but that she put them on, return to the street, and reenter the house, this time removing the coat and hanging it properly.
>
> —E. R. GUTHRIE[3]

[3] *The Psychology of Learning* (New York: Harper & Row, 1952), p. 18.

The mother in this example did not teach her daughter anything the daughter did not know how to do. There is no (22)________ shaping in this example.

There is no operant shaping in this example. The daughter knew how to hang up her coat and hat. The problem was that she usually (23)________ hang up her coat and hat when she entered the house.

The girl in the example did not hang up her things after her mother gave her lectures, or rewards, or punishments. The girl began to hang up her coat and hat whenever she came in, only after her mother on several occasions made her hang them up in the presence of the entire sequence of stimulus-(24)________ normally present when the daughter entered the house wearing her coat and hat.

All of the stimulus-actions normally present for the daughter when she entered the house wearing her coat and hat became associated with hanging up her coat and hat after the mother followed the psychologist's advice. *This was not respondent conditioning.* Hanging up coat and hat is certainly not respondent. *Neither is it* (25)________ *conditioning.*

Operant conditioning is the name for the process by which a behavioral situation comes to produce a certain type of operant more and more frequently *when such operants are followed by* (26)________.

There was no specific reinforcing consequence of hanging up her coat and hat to encourage the girl to do so. Thus this is not an example of operant conditioning. We need a label for this kind of learning. Guthrie calls it associative (27)____________.

MORE EXAMPLES OF ASSOCIATIVE LEARNING

In his writings Guthrie points out many examples of *associative learning* of discriminative stimuli for operants in which the operants are not necessarily followed by reinforcing consequences.

> If we wish to teach a dog to come when he is called, our method will be to get him to come to us by hook or crook. There are no rules for this except what we know of dogs in general. We may hold up a bone, start running away from the dog, pull him toward us on a check line, or use any device which experience has suggested. While he is coming we speak the dog's name. If we take care not to speak the name on any occasion when we foresee that he will not come—when he is, for instance, chasing a cat or gnawing a bone (when we believe an unwanted response is dominant)—we can readily establish a stable conditioned response. We say that the dog "knows" his name. If we are so misguided as to try to call him back from the pursuit of a passing car before we have insured the effectiveness of calling, we have reconditioned the dog and made his name a signal for chasing cars, not for coming to us.
>
> The skilled trainer uses the dog's name only when the prompt response is highly certain. If the response fails, he does not repeat the name, but uses his practical knowledge to remove the causes of failure or waits until the cause is removed. The dog may have been occupied in looking at another dog or watching a passer-by. The trainer waits until he has the dog's attention before he

> repeats the name. Otherwise the name tends to become a cue for looking at the passerby and noticing other dogs.
>
> It is on exactly the same ground that the student officer is cautioned never to give a command that he is not confident will be obeyed. If the command is followed by acts other than those commanded, the command becomes merely a cue for disobedience and the officer loses his authority.
>
> —E. R. GUTHRIE[4]

Guthrie gives many such examples in his writings of the importance of contiguity of stimulus and response. Many students will be able to think of other examples for themselves. Parents find that little children will go to sleep much more easily when a ritual is followed that has been associated with bedtime and sleep. Students find that they study more efficiently at a desk that is never used for anything but study and never associated with daydreaming or other responses incompatible to study.

All kinds of conditioning seem to require that cues (CSs and S^Ds) occur in contiguity with a response. *In contiguity with* means (28)"______________."

In contiguity with means "at the same time as." But is contiguity in time enough? Contiguity between CS and response seems to be enough for (29)______________ conditioning.

[4] *The Psychology of Learning, op. cit.,* pp. 40 ff.

Respondent conditioning is explained quite well by Guthrie's theory. As we have seen above, many instances of associative learning of operants are also explained quite well by Guthrie's theory. Operant conditioning, however, involves more than associative learning. There is no reinforcing consequence in many instances of associative learning. Operant conditioning seems to be explained more satisfactorily after we add one further principle which helps explain the effects of reinforcing consequences.

PRINCIPLE G: INTENSITY OF RESPONSE

When a response is intense, the behavioral situation of the individual is constricted. More muscles and glands participate in the total response and fewer unrelated responses occur.

Fewer responses means fewer stimulus-actions to become cues, but each stimulus-action is conditioned to all of the individual respondents and all of the operant patterns of muscle-twitch that do occur.

"Operant conditioning" is the name for the process by which a behavioral situation comes to produce a certain type of operant more and more frequently when such operants are followed by (30)____________ (*discriminative stimuli* or *reinforcing consequences*?).

Guthrie explains how reinforcing consequences of an operant make the individual more likely to emit that operant in the future. In order to explain how reinforcing consequences work we must use *Principle F: Contiguity and* (31)__________, and *Principle G:* (32)__________ *of Response.*

Principle F: Contiguity and Operants and Principle G: Intensity of Response can be used to explain the effects of reinforcing consequences. The quotation at the beginning of Lesson 13 will summarize how reinforcement works according to Guthrie's theory.

LESSON TEST: ANSWER THE FOLLOWING QUESTIONS WITHOUT LOOKING BACK AT THE LESSON:

1. An understanding of associative learning can be very useful to any student (or teacher, or parent!). For example, some psychologists advise students *never* to do anything but study at their study desk and to leave the study desk whenever they find it hard to concentrate or decide to do anything other than study. Many students have found this hard to do, but some students with low averages have raised their semester averages by as much as a full letter grade when they did it. Why does the contiguity theory predict this might work? (Studying is operant but this is not operant conditioning, and not operant shaping.)
2. Write out *Principle F: Contiguity and Operants.*

3. Write out *Principle* G: *Intensity of Response.*

CHECK YOUR ANSWERS (OR EXCHANGE ANSWERS AND CHECK) BY LOOKING BACK AT THE LESSON. CAREFULLY CORRECT EVERY MISTAKE OR OMISSION.

LESSON 13

Reinforcement and Punishment

[Estimated time: 30 minutes]

States of excitement play an important part in learning because they intensify action, and by intensifying action alter its results and bring new stimulation. Excitement is often the essential condition of adaptation and learning because it means vigorous action and new behavior.

. . . .

There must be first some situation that produces activity, some maintained source of restlessness and uneasy behavior. In the ensuing activity some action eventually removes this maintaining stimulus for excitement. *This action remains associated with the distressing situation because, once the distressing situation is removed, it can acquire no new associations.* We thus tend strongly to learn actions that remove us from trouble and distress. The stimuli may be within us, as in the case of hunger. The act of eating does away with our restlessness and sometimes with its source. Eating becomes our cure for that particular form of distress.

—E. R. GUTHRIE[1]

[1] "Conditioning: A Theory of Learning in Terms of Stimulus, Response, and Association," *The Psychology of Learning, Yearbook XLI, Part II* (Chicago: National Society for the Study of Education, 1942), pp. 22, 44.

In the quotation above, Guthrie emphasizes the importance of motivation. The first paragraph of the quotation says the same thing said by Principle G: (1)________ of Response.

According to Principle G, when a response is intense, the behavioral situation of the individual is (2)________ (*constricted* or *expanded*?).

When an individual is excited, his behavioral situation is constricted—that is, he tends to concentrate his attention, and (3)____________ (*fewer* or *more*?) unrelated responses occur.

Fewer unrelated responses occur when an individual's behavior is being maintained (that is driven or motivated) by such things as electric shock stimulation or internal conditions resulting from extended absence of food or water. According to the Principles of Contiguity (Principles A and F), every response pattern that does occur is immediately and completely associated with all of the stimulus-actions in the (4)____________ situation at that time.

Every response pattern is associated with the entire behavioral situation at each moment. At the next moment, if the response pattern changes, this changed response pattern will be associated with the entire behavioral situation at that moment. If a stimulus-pattern is associated with one response pattern and then later is associated with another response pattern, it will lose its connection to the first pattern according to Principle E: (5)________ (*Intensity* or *Permanency*?) of Conditioning.

The principle of Permanency of Conditioning is the key to Guthrie's explanation for the process of reinforcement—Guthrie's explanation of how reinforcing consequences affect (6)__________ (*operants* or *respondents*?).

Reinforcing consequences of an operant increase the probability that such operants will be repeated in future similar situations. According to Guthrie in the quotation at the beginning of this lesson, an event that *removes a maintaining stimulus* will act as a (7)__________ consequence for the operants it follows.

Reinforcing consequences that follow an operant increase the probability that that operant will be repeated in future similar behavioral situations. Reinforcing consequences reinforce because they (8)__________ (*present* or *remove*?) maintaining stimuli.

Reinforcing consequences remove (9)__________ stimuli.

Reinforcing consequences reinforce operants by removing the maintaining stimuli for the operant.

TO MAKE THIS CLEAR, CAREFULLY REREAD THE QUOTATION AT THE BEGINNING OF THIS LESSON.

REINFORCEMENT

There are two kinds of agents that provide events that act as reinforcing consequences. An agent whose *termination* is a reinforcing consequence is called a (10)____________ (*negative* reinforcer or *positive* reinforcer?).

Negative reinforcers such as electric shock are agents whose termination is a reinforcing consequence. Electric shock is an example of the type of distressing stimuli that Guthrie calls (11)____________ stimuli.

Electric shock is a maintaining stimulus.

An agent whose *onset* is a reinforcing consequence is called a (12)____________ reinforcer.

A positive reinforcer such as food, is an agent whose onset is a reinforcing consequence. Food is not a maintaining stimulus. Food is a means for terminating certain (13)____________ stimuli.

Eating food removes certain maintaining stimuli. Presentation of food is most reinforcing when the individual is "hungry," when he has not had anything to eat for a while. Eating the food does away with internal maintaining stimuli that arise when we have not eaten over a period of time.

Reinforcement is a *process*. Reinforcement is the process involved when a reinforcer provides a reinforcing consequence. A reinforcer is (14)________ (*an agent* or *an event*?). A reinforcing consequence is (15)________ (*an agent, an event* or *a process*?). Reinforcement is (16)____________ (*an agent, an event*, or *a process*?).

A reinforcer is an agent; a reinforcing consequence is an event; (17)____________ is a process.

Most theories of learning agree that we learn to repeat operants that are reinforced. Guthrie's contiguity theory proposes an explanation for why the process of (18)____________ works.

Reinforcement works because the reinforcing consequence that follows the operant (19)__________. (Answer in your own words on the back of your answer sheet, then compare your answer to Guthrie's explanation in the quotation at the beginning of this lesson *and change your answer if you wish.*)

One way of rephrasing Guthrie's words is to say that reinforcement works because the reinforcing consequence removes the maintaining stimuli and thus prevents the individual from associating any other new response to the stimulus pattern that was present just before the response was made.

PUNISHMENT

The process of reinforcement takes place when a response occurs in a situation, and an event that happens immediately after the response makes it likely that that response will be repeated the next time the individual is in a similar situation. Punishment is quite a different process.

Punishment is not exactly the opposite of reinforcement. In the process of punishment, as opposed to the process of reinforcement, the opposite kind of events follows the response, but the result (20)____________ (*is* or *is not*?) always the opposite.

We define reinforcement as the occurrence of a reinforcing consequence. There are two kinds of reinforcing consequences: the termination of a (21)____________ reinforcer, and the onset of a (22)____________ reinforcer.

Reinforcement is the termination of a negative reinforcer or the onset of a positive reinforcer. Punishment is the (23)____________ (*opposite* or *same*?) operation.

Punishment is just the opposite operation from reinforcement. Punishment is the (24)__________ of a negative reinforcer or the (25)__________ of a positive reinforcer.

DEFINITION: Punishment *is the process involved when the onset of a negative reinforcer or the termination of a positive reinforcer follows a response.*

Such things as the onset of something that gives pain and the removal of food are punisments. The problem posed by punishment is that the effects of punishment are so varied. Punishment sometimes seems to reduce the probability of repetition of responses that it follows. On the other hand, sometimes punishment actually seems to act as a reinforcing consequence! Dashiell gives some simple, everyday examples of this:

> . . . Who has not, at some time or other, enjoyed enhancing a painful twinge in a hollow tooth by perversely thrusting his tongue into the cavity? Or perhaps as a small child has refused to pull out a nail coming through the sole of his shoe, so that he might experience some titillation from the pain receptors of the wound? Higher levels of daily living furnish plenty of examples. The worker who toils on despite aching fingers and throbbing head; the impecunious student who pursues his college studies in the face of trying financial difficulties; the army recruit who chooses combat service though he suspects what horrors may be in store; and dozens of less dramatic incidents of every day when one takes the right turn though

it would be easier and pleasanter to turn left and go fishing. . . .

JOHN FREDERICK DASHIELL[2]

In this quotation Dashiell gives several examples of punishment in the form of *onset* of a negative reinforcer acting as a (26)____________ consequence.

Reinforcements by reinforcing consequences such as the onset of positive reinforcers or termination of negative reinforcers *always increase* the probability of repetition of operants that they follow. The *probability* of repetition of operants *is not*, *however*, *always decreased* or reduced by (27)____________.

Punishment is the process involved when the *onset* of a (28)____________ reinforcer or the *termination* of a (29)____________ follows an operant.

The problem of the effects of punishment and the reason for the varied effects is very complex. Guthrie summarizes his position as follows:

> . . . what is learned will be what is done—and what is done in intense feeling is usually something different from what was being done. Sitting on tacks does not discourage learning. It encourages one in learning to do something else than sit. It is . . . the specific action caused

[2] *Fundamentals of General Psychology* (New York: Houghton Mifflin, 1949), p. 346.

by punishment that determines what will be learned. In training a dog to jump through a hoop, the effectiveness of punishment depends on where it is applied, front or rear. It is what the punishment makes the dog *do* that counts. . . .

. . . Punishment achieves its effects not by taking away strength from the physiological basis of the connection . . . , but by forcing the animal or the child to do something different and thus establishing inhibitory conditioning of unwanted habit. Punishment is effective *only in the presence of cues for the bad habit.*

—E. R. GUTHRIE[3]

LESSON TEST: AFTER YOU HAVE COMPLETED THIS LESSON, ANSWER THE FOLLOWING QUESTIONS WITHOUT LOOKING BACK AT THE LESSON:

1. Guthrie formulated his theory before Skinner suggested classifying behavior into "operants" and "respondents." Guthrie does stress the difference between "movements" (responses of individual muscles and glands) and "acts" combinations of movements defined in terms of the effect of the total combination of movements upon the environment). Guthrie's "movements" are ___________ (*operants* or *respondents*?). Guthrie's "act's" are ___________ (*operants* or *respondents*?).

2. Match the two following lists: reinforcement, positive reinforcer, reinforcing consequence; agent, event, process.

3. Define "punishment" as it is defined in this lesson.

[3] *The Psychology of Learning* (New York: Harper & Row, 1952), pp. 132 ff.

4. In what way is punishment not the opposite of reinforcement?
5. According to Guthrie's theory, how (given in his own words at the beginning of this lesson) does reinforcement work?

CHECK YOUR ANSWERS (OR EXCHANGE ANSWERS AND CHECK) BY LOOKING BACK AT THE LESSON. CAREFULLY CORRECT EVERY MISTAKE OR OMISSION.

PROJECT

IV

Experimental Analysis: Probability Matching

> . . . over a series of trials in which two alternative reinforcing events occur with fixed probabilities, the subject's probability of predicting a given event tends to approach ("match") the actual probability of the event. Two groups of investigators found this result of special interest: adherents of traditional law of effect, or classic economic doctrine, because they felt such a result should not occur; and investigators working with the, then new, statistical learning theories, because they felt such a result is precisely what should be expected.
>
> —W. K. Estes[1]

You are shown a deck of playing cards and told that they will be thoroughly shuffled and then turned face up one by one. You are to guess each time whether the next card will be black or red before the face of the card is exposed. A standard bridge deck contains fifty-two cards, twenty-six red cards and twenty-six black cards. If you guess black every time, you will be correct 50 percent of the time. If you guess red every time, you will be correct 50 percent of the time. If you randomly guess black and red, you will also be correct an average of half the time.

[1] "Learning Theory," *Annual Review of Psychology*, Vol. 13 (Palo Alto: Annual Reviews, Inc. 1962), p. 131.

If someone has "stacked the deck" by removing all of the red cards, you will always be correct when you predict that the next card will be black. You will never be correct when you guess red. If you randomly guess black and red, you will be correct an average of half of the time.

What if the deck of cards contains three red cards for every black card? Now, if you guess black every time you will be correct one time out of four on the average (25 percent of the time). If you guess red every time, you will be correct 75 percent of the time, on the average. Once again, if you randomly guess black and red, you will be correct an average of half of the time.

If there are more black cards than red cards in the deck, the strategy of always guessing black will "pay off" more often than any other strategy. This is the way to maximize your number of correct guesses. If your guesses correspond to the proportion of black and red cards (such as guessing black four out of five times when there are actually four black cards to every red card in the deck), you will not be correct as often as you will if you always guess black. For example, if 80 percent of the cards are black and you always guess black, you will be correct 80 percent of the time. If 80 percent of the cards are black and you guess black 80 percent of the time, you will be correct an average of 64 percent of the time. Of course, this is better than being correct only half of the time (as you would be if you guessed completely randomly).

As W. K. Estes says in the quotation at the beginning of this project, both classic doctrine in economics and the traditional law of effect in psychology predict that an individual will tend to make the choices that will maximize the probability of being correct or winning.

Statistical learning theories, on the other hand, predict

that on the average an individual's guesses will tend to match the proportion of times the guesses have been correct in the past. Thus, if red has been correct 60 percent of the time in the past, an individual will tend to guess red 60 percent of the time. In terms of contiguity theory as we have been developing it in these lessons, about 60 percent of the stimulus-actions in the behavioral situation will have become cues for the response of saying "red."

Here is a summary of the guesses made by five of the people participating in one study. These subjects were shown cards from a pack of sixty playing cards which actually contained forty-eight black cards and twelve red cards (80 percent black cards). The subjects were shown the cards one by one through the deck. Then the deck was shuffled while they watched, and they were shown the cards one by one again.

	Number of Responses (Predictions) of "Black" in Each Twenty Cards					
	Number:					
Subject (S)	1–20	21–40	41–60	61–80	81–100	101–120
A	8	10	15	13	17	14
B	11	13	11	14	15	16
C	4	10	15	17	15	15
D	16	9	16	17	20	20
E	7	10	9	12	13	11
Average (arithmetic mean) number of guesses "Black" for each set of twenty guesses	9.2	10.4	13.2	14.6	16.0	15.2
Percentage of guesses "Black"	46	52	66	73	80	76

As a whole, the results for these five subjects support the prediction of statistical learning theory (and of contiguity theory). Subject D, however, maximized his number of correct guesses by always guessing black on the last forty cards. Subject E, on the other hand, seems to have guessed fairly randomly.

PURPOSE: To make a small test of the prediction that *S*'s proportion of guesses in a two-choice situation will tend to match the probability of the events rather than tend to maximize the number of correct guesses.

MATERIALS: Two decks of bridge-playing cards. One deck with the aces of diamonds and hearts and all of the spades and clubs removed (leaving twenty-four red cards). A second deck with the aces of diamonds, hearts, clubs, and all of the spades removed (leaving twenty-four red cards and twelve black cards). The two decks together will total sixty cards, forty-eight red cards and twelve black cards (80 percent red). The cards must be carefully and thoroughly shuffled together each time before they are used.

SUBJECTS: To make a reasonable test you should try this project with at least five different people who know nothing about the project or its purpose.

PROCEDURE: Read the following instructions to your subject:

> This is an experiment for my psychology course for which I have asked your help. I have here a stack of cards. Some of them are black and some are red. Please ask no questions and make no comments except to tell me each time whether you think the next card will be a black one or a red one. I will then write down your pre-

diction and the actual color of the card and show you the card. The experiment will be completely explained in detail after you have taken all of the tests. Do you understand what you are to do?

Go through the deck entirely. Then shuffle the cards carefully and go through the deck again.

REPORT:

Part I. Write what happened when you tried this project. Make a table similar to the one above.

Part II. Another example of experiments that classic doctrine in economics and the traditional law of effect find difficult to explain are the various experiments on "intermittent reinforcement." Studies of probability matching and of intermittent reinforcement have many social science applications that are not yet widely recognized. Go to a library (or consult a recent introductory psychology textbook) and look up "intermittent reinforcement" (sometimes called "partial reinforcement"). Why are the results of intermittent reinforcement experiments difficult for classic economic doctrine to explain? How are these studies related to the phenomena of probability matching?

COMMENT: We expect people to act in such a way that in the long run, or at least in the short run, they will get the most reward (that is, the most reinforcement) for the least effort. In probability matching situations and in intermittent reinforcement situations (in the gambling casino as well as in the psychology laboratory) people do not do what will bring the most reward for the least effort. This fact is worth pondering.

Appendix

Prepublication Research and Revisions

Over a period of seven years more than one thousand students studied various preliminary versions of these lessons. Each lesson was tested and revised and tested again until the number of "correct" answers by students studying the final form of the lesson was over 95 percent (and, as much as possible, no item in a lesson was answered "incorrectly" by more than 10 percent of the students). After several lessons were completed, further revisions were guided by comments of reviewers and by analysis of student answers on examinations covering the lesson material.

While the lessons were being written and revised, experiments were done to answer questions about the best way to present the material and the success of different formats and different ways of studying the lessons. Three of these studies are worth reporting.

1. Programmed lessons usually provide the student with "correct" or "comparison" answers against which to check their own responses to the items. The comparison answer for an item may be given on the next page (see R. Glaser, L. E. Homme, and J. L. Evans, "An evaluation of textbooks in terms of learning principles"; A. A. Lumsdaine, and R. Glaser, (eds.) *Teaching machines and programmed learning: a source book,* Washington: N.E.A., 1960, pp. 437–445). Or the comparison answer may be placed beside or below the item (see J. A. Barlow, J. Gilpin, D. D. Hedberg, and A. Palmer, "A scanning principle for auto-instructional devices," *J. exp. anal.*

Behav. [1961], *4*: 360). The first forms of several of the lessons in this book used a third format. Instead of the comparison answers being placed on the next page or set off beside or below the question, the comparison answer is contained in the next item in capital letters (see J. A. Barlow, "Conversational chaining in teaching machine programs," *Psychol. Rep.* [1960], 7:187–193).

In the spring of 1962 at Emory University, students in Introductory Psychology studied five lessons (over 150 "frames" or individual items) of this book (as the lessons were set up at that time). Three formats were compared: (a) comparison answer given in capital letters within the context of the next item (the original conversational format); (b) exactly the same items without any capitalization or emphasis on the comparison answer as contained in the next item but with the comparison answer presented beside each item in a column in the right margin (scanning format); (c) exactly the same items without any capitalization or comparison answers in the next item and without any comparison answers beside the items (modified conversational format without emphasis on response confirmation). Students were instructed to cover the items with a piece of paper and to read and answer each item before looking at the next item. Students studying format (b) were instructed to cover the answer column with a piece of paper and not to expose an answer to an item until they had answered the item.

The success of each of these three formats seemed to be approximately the same as indicated by the number of "correct" answers given by students as they studied and by performance on an examination covering the lessons. When all three formats were shown to the students and they were asked which format they preferred, there was some preference for format (c)—i.e., no emphasis at all upon the comparison answers. Since the time of this study, format (c) has been the normal format for these lessons.

In recent editions two further changes have been made. First, when responses acceptable to the author ("correct") are consistently given by almost every student, the confirming word, sentence, or phrase, in the next item is usually omitted if this does not in any way distort the item. Thus in some lessons in the present book, as many as half of the items never have the "correct" item confirmed in any way. Second, in a few specific instances it seems important to emphasize that certain answers are acceptable and other answers are not acceptable (even though students tend to give the correct answer). In such cases a list of item numbers and the "correct" answers are given after the set of items.

2. In the spring of 1966 at the Indiana University Regional Campus in Fort Wayne, freshmen in the classes of T. L. Engle studied these lessons (as the lessons were at that time) in two formats. Some of the students were given the lessons to study in narrative form (the blanks all filled in, item numbers removed, and spaces between the items removed so that the lessons became similar in appearance to any conventionally written narrative). Other students studied the lessons "with blanks" (i.e., as they appear in this book) and were required to turn in their answers. Those who studied the narrative form did not do as well on the examination covering the lessons. (69 students studied the narrative form and on a multiple-choice test achieved a mean score of 54.4 with a standard deviation of 15.5. 102 students studied the lessons with blanks and achieved a mean score of 62.2 with a standard deviation of 12.3. The resulting t of 3.7 is significant at well beyond the one percent level.)

Mean Test Score as a Function of Study Method and SAT Verbal Score

	SAT under 500	SAT over 500
Given narrative form to read	45.3 (n = 22)	60.9 (n = 14)
Given lessons with blanks to fill in	61.4 (n = 37)	69.2 (n = 14)

Examination of the scores of those freshmen in T. L. Engle's classes for whom Scholastic Aptitude Test scores were available indicates that filling in the blanks as they study is particularly helpful for students with SAT verbal scores of less than 500.

3. In the fall of 1966 at Hope College, freshmen in the class of F. Phillip Van Eyl studied these lessons (as these lessons were set up at that time). These students were given an appendix with the lessons. In the appendix were listed one or more acceptable answers for each item in the lessons. Students were instructed to complete a lesson and then compare their answers to those in the appendix and carefully re-examine any item for which they did not give a "correct" answer. Inadvertently, two of the answers given for Lesson 6 were entirely unrelated to the items with the corresponding numbers in the lesson. Of the fifty-two students who turned in their answers to all of the lessons, thirteen turned in sets of answers that included these completely inappropriate answers for Lesson 6. A comparison of the examination scores of these students confirms the conclusion reached in Fort Wayne: it is important for a student to write out his own answers as he studies the lessons. The students who seem to have "cheated" by copying the answers from the appendix must have, at least, read the lessons, as their scores are much superior to scores of students taking the same examination before studying the program. The mean score for those who seem to have done the lessons as instructed was 39.0 correct out of fifty-three questions. The mean score for those who copied was 35.2. (The resulting t ratio of 2.18 is significant at the 5 percent level.)

CONCLUSION

Some freshmen dream of professors who pleasantly and painlessly fill students with wisdom. Acceptable assignments in this dream are those that entertain and amuse without "busywork." Textbooks are always clear, concise, and complete, so that, if necessary, a student can conveniently read one for review the night before an examination.

Some professors dream of freshmen who always eagerly and joyfully strive for new knowledge. Acceptable work in this dream is work that shows initiative and effort beyond the assignments. Students are diligent junior colleagues continuously participating in the eternal quest for knowledge.

The students' dream, I am afraid, is a delusion. The professors' dream, furthermore, is a phantasy. Despite what seemed to be the prophecies and promises of some early promoters, programmed instruction does not seem to show much promise of giving any real substance to these dreams.

A validated program is a book that has been student-tested and revised until it is effective. It does not teach. That is, it does teach if the student does the work. It does not by itself persuade the student that the time and effort required for mastery are worth his while.

> The analogy of the teacher's work to that of the gardener or farmer seems a good one. . . . The gardener makes all possible arrangements for the growth of his plants. . . . But he never once assumes that he is going to do the growing for the plants. . . .
>
> Similarly, the teacher makes all possible arrangements for growth to take place, but in the final analysis he has to admit that the learner must himself do the growing.
>
> —EARL C. KELLEY AND MARIE I. RASEY[1]

FURTHER VALIDATION

The author plans to prepare complete reports on the above experiments in testing and revising the lessons and to submit these reports to appropriate professional journals. A teacher's manual is planned, which will include a copy of the criteria test, a report on the scores obtained by students before and after they have studied the published version of the program, and other information that may be of value to a teacher planning to use this program. Inquiries concerning this material should be directed to Psychology Editor, College Department, Harper & Row, Publishers, Inc., 49 E. 33rd St., N.Y., N.Y. 10016.

[1] *Education and the Nature of Man* (New York: Harper & Row, 1952), p. 75.

68 69 70 7 6 5 4 3 2 1